The Civil War

A Captivating Guide to the American Civil War and Its Impact on the History of the United States

© **Copyright 2018**

All Rights Reserved. No part of this book may be reproduced in any form without permission in writing from the author. Reviewers may quote brief passages in reviews.

Disclaimer: No part of this publication may be reproduced or transmitted in any form or by any means, mechanical or electronic, including photocopying or recording, or by any information storage and retrieval system, or transmitted by email without permission in writing from the publisher.

While all attempts have been made to verify the information provided in this publication, neither the author nor the publisher assumes any responsibility for errors, omissions or contrary interpretations of the subject matter herein.

This book is for entertainment purposes only. The views expressed are those of the author alone and should not be taken as expert instruction or commands. The reader is responsible for his or her own actions.

Adherence to all applicable laws and regulations, including international, federal, state and local laws governing professional licensing, business practices, advertising and all other aspects of doing business in the US, Canada, UK, or any other jurisdiction is the sole responsibility of the purchaser or reader.

Neither the author nor the publisher assumes any responsibility or liability whatsoever on the behalf of the purchaser or reader of these materials. Any perceived slight of any individual or organization is purely unintentional.

Free Bonus from Captivating History (Available for a Limited time)

Hi History Lovers!

Now you have a chance to join our exclusive history list so you can get your first history ebook for free as well as discounts and a potential to get more history books for free! Simply visit the link below to join.

Captivatinghistory.com/ebook

Also, make sure to follow us on:

Twitter: @Captivhistory

Facebook: Captivating History:@captivatinghistory

Contents

INTRODUCTION 1
CHAPTER 1 – AN UNEASY NATION 3
    STEPS TO SECESSION 3
    UNCLE TOM'S CABIN PUBLISHED 5
    NEBRASKA-KANSAS ACT 5
    LINCOLN WINS A CLOSE RACE 7
CHAPTER 2 – THE FOUNDATION CRACKS 9
    SOUTH CAROLINA LEADS SECESSION 9
    FORT MOULTRIE 10
    CONFEDERATE CONSTITUTION 11
    A NATION AND A STATE DIVIDED 11
    THE PRESIDENTS 12
        Jefferson Davis 12
        Abraham Lincoln 13
    LINCOLN'S INAUGURATION 15
CHAPTER 3 – THE FIRST SHOT 22
    FORT SUMTER 22
    THE SOUTH RISES 23
CHAPTER 4 – WELCOME TO WAR 26

An Introduction of the Generals 27
    Ulysses S. Grant *27*
    Robert E. Lee *28*
    William Tecumseh Sherman *30*
    Thomas "Stonewall" Jackson *31*
First Battle of Bull Run 33
Monitor vs. Merrimack 34

CHAPTER 5 – BLOODY DAYS 37
Battle of Shiloh 37
The Seven Days Campaign 39
Second Battle of Bull Run 41
The Push North 42
Antietam 43

CHAPTER 6 – PROCLAIMING FREEDOM 45
Preliminary Emancipation 45
Fredericksburg 46
Emancipation Proclamation 48
Impressment and Military Draft 49

CHAPTER 7 – THE WAR LOOKS GRIM 51
Chancellorsville 51
Gettysburg 53

CHAPTER 8 – TURNING THE TIDE 55
Vicksburg 55
Battle of Chickamauga 56
Gettysburg Address 57
Battle of Wilderness 58
Siege of Petersburg 59

CHAPTER 9 – THE FINAL FIGHT 61
Sherman Burns Atlanta 61

- Sherman's March to the Sea 62
- Fall of Richmond 63

CHAPTER 10 – REUNITED 65
- 13th Amendment Ends Slavery 65
- Second Lincoln Inaugural 66
- Lincoln Shot 68
- Lincoln Dies 69
- Johnston Surrenders 70
- The End of The Confederacy 70
- My Brother, My Prisoner 71

CHAPTER 11 – POST-WAR AMERICA 73
- Union Reunited 73
- Reconstruction (1865-1877) 74

CONCLUSION 77

Introduction

No other war in the history of the United States has sparked as much debate and conflict as the American Civil War. For over 150 years, the story of the Civil War has been a source of contention, confusion, and even contempt in American life. Even today, the American public cannot agree on the causes of the Civil War, never mind its lessons or legacy.

More Americans died in the Civil War than in WWI, WWII, and Vietnam combined. The war not only put Americans against Americans but family against family, neighbor against neighbor, friend against friend. The conflict between the Union and the Confederacy still runs deep in some parts of the United States. Indeed, the fundamental questions of the Civil War—questions about racial (in)equality, the rights of citizenship, and the role of government—remain hot debates today. In many ways, the war that claimed over 600,000 American lives a century and a half ago is still the biggest battle being waged on American soil.

By understanding the causes, course, and repercussions of the Civil War, we can better grasp the underlying issues in the current American political climate, and realize the long-lasting scars on the United States population. As we cover the events leading up to the Civil War, we will explore the cracks in the foundation of the Union, the sparks leading to rebellion, and the discord amongst the citizens of the United States. The story of the war itself is one of horrific suffering, as well as jubilant liberation. The period after the war, known as Reconstruction, was a bold experiment in racial equality, and was resisted with equal ferocity by the Old Confederacy as was any Union advance at Gettysburg or Antietam.

Among the American public, if not among historians, the jury is still out on the meaning of the Civil War. Was the Civil War a war fought to keep the Union together? Was it fought to free slaves and end the blight of servitude against the will of the people who were in bondage? Was it a war of Northern aggression, justified through Republican ideals and with disregard to the Southern way of life? Depending on the year, election cycle, and individual perspective, an American might describe the war as one of the greatest achievements, or greatest tragedies, in American history. Through this exploration of the Civil War, we will learn about the origins and impacts of these diverse perspectives. We will also learn how modern historians explain the Civil War, especially when their ideas differ from those held by the general public.

The Civil War is a story full of struggle and despair, and one that is full of hope. It is a story from the American past that has a strong hold on our present. It may even be a story that could change our future.

Chapter 1 – An Uneasy Nation

Tension over slavery and the expansion of slavery into prospective states and territories had become a hot topic of debate. While many believed that the Constitution was clear on the expansion of slavery, there were some who saw their fortunes hanging in the balance as the United States expanded further west, opening new territories and offering new opportunities for citizens of the Union. With many taking a pro- or anti- stance regarding it, the topic of slavery would dominate American politics for the next three decades.

Steps to Secession

The northern and southern states had been at odds about slavery since the formation of the United States. Each state's representation in the United States Congress is determined by its population. When the country was being formed, they took a census of the population of the states to determine the number of representatives that each would be allocated.

The Southern states wanted each slave to be counted as a citizen. The Northern states opposed. They argued that if the slaves did not have the rights of other American citizens, they should not be counted in the population. The first piece of slavery-related legislation ever adopted by America was due to this disagreement.

Coined "The Great Compromise," the legislation required that three of every five slaves be counted toward the total population. This gave southern states more power in terms of the number of their legislators, but not as much power as they would have if all slaves were counted.

While the United States was seeing growth in industry and manufacturing in the North, the South was booming with large-scale agriculture service through slavery. The two largest money-making crops in the South were tobacco and cotton, both of which relied on manual labor in the form of slaves to be profitable. The growing abolitionist movement in the North was pushing for slavery to be banned in new territories. This brought about a deep-seated fear in Southerners that their way of life, and therefore their economy, were at risk. Subsequently, these factors created tensions amongst the North and South.

The South lamented that they were the financial backbone of the North. Southern money paid for necessities and luxuries from the North. Southerners purchased equipment and clothing from the North while simultaneously shipping their cotton North to be processed, and their children North to be educated. The North had a stranglehold on the Southern economy and had the potential to cripple them at will.

In 1819 as westward expansion advanced, a measure was brought to Congress which sought to prohibit slavery in the Missouri Territory. This measure would limit further expansion of cotton farming, as well as tip the balance of Congressional power even further into the hand of the North, since another anti-slavery state entering the union would leave 12 anti-slavery states versus 11 pro-slavery.[i] A compromise was needed.

In 1820 Congress came together and created the Missouri Compromise. The Missouri Compromise would allow Missouri to enter the Union as a slave state and Maine would be entered as a free state, thus allowing 12 states for each side of the slavery issue and keeping power balanced, but the balance was weak.[ii]

In 1846 the Mexican War threatened to upend the hard work of the Missouri Compromise as a measure was introduced banning "slavery or involuntary servitude" in any territory acquired after the war. The mention of banning slavery riled up the South and threatened an already tense peace.[iii]

Uncle Tom's Cabin Published

In 1852, with the dignity of slavery being questioned in the North and feelings of oppression and misunderstanding permeating the south, *Uncle Tom's Cabin* was published. It was met with shock by all United States citizens, but for very different reasons.

In the north, abolitionists clung to the book as their justification for ending slavery in the country. Northerners were astonished by the story of a slave who held great Christian fortitude while being sold like livestock, caring for a sick child with no means to do so, and finally being beaten to death for formulating a plan to free slaves.

Southerners were outraged because they thought the book was an unfair representation of a slave's life on a plantation in the South. Their main argument was that blacks were sub-human and did not have the capacity to feel pain or even love. If slaves were the same class as livestock, they had the right to beat a slave that wouldn't work just as they have the right to whip a mule that doesn't pull a plow. The book added even more tinder to an already huge bonfire that was about to be ignited.

Nebraska-Kansas Act

In 1854 the Nebraska-Kansas Act was passed creating the states of Nebraska and Kansas. With the expansion of the American West came the question of expanding slavery into the new territories. Two factions emerged in Kansas; the "Free-Staters" who wanted Kansas to be a free state without slavery and the "Border Ruffians" who wanted Kansas to enter the Union as a slave state.[iv]

Even the political discourse over whether states would be free or slave-holding became violent. In 1856, Congressman Charles Sumner from Massachusetts was giving an anti-slavery speech on the floor of the House. He began calling Southern slave owners pimps and made derogatory references about the physical handicaps of Mississippi Congressman Preston Brooks' brother.

Brooks became enraged and stormed across the aisle attacking Sumner with his cane. Other pro-slavery congressmen kept people from stopping the beating by waving firearms at would-be interveners. The bludgeoning left Sumner unconscious on the house floor. It took three years for him to recover from the wounds inflicted.

What started as a hotbed political debate quickly turned into more severe actions including ballot rigging, intimidation, and violence. These tactics, practiced by both groups, led to confrontations and an outbreak of violence which culminated in a conflict known as Bleeding Kansas. With this bloodshed already becoming an issue in territories of the United States, many wondered what would happen if the election swung for the abolitionists.

The escalation of conflict between abolitionists and those who were pro-slavery was further strained in 1857 as the Supreme Court ruled against Dred Scott in *Dred Scott v. Sanford*. The ruling stated, "A free negro of the African race, whose ancestors were brought to this country and sold as slaves, is not a "citizen" within the meaning of the Constitution of the United States." And that "The Constitution of the United States recognizes slaves as property and pledges the Federal Government to protect it. And Congress cannot exercise any more authority over property of that description than it may constitutionally exercise over property of any other kind."[v]

The ruling in *Dred Scott* had further ramifications and further emboldened the South to expand slavery since slaves would remain enslaved regardless of which territory they were in. This angered many in the North who had fought hard to abolish slavery by fair and lawful means. The Southern victory in the Scott case was the final straw for many in the North. The approaching race for President would determine how that ruling would be enforced, and the result of the election would turn out to be the straw to break the back of the uneasy truce.

Lincoln Wins A Close Race

This ruling did more than just embolden the South. In 1859 John Brown planned to raid Virginia to free slaves held there, lead them on to a larger raid, and then bring about a general slave insurrection in that state. Before he could put his plan into action, he needed to obtain more weapons. On October 16, 1859, John Brown led a raid against the Federal armory in Harpers Ferry, Virginia. The raid was considered a success as the twenty-one men (16 whites, four free blacks, and one escaped slave) took the Federal armory without a single shot.[vi] This act by abolitionists emboldened both sides towards conflict. The North saw the possibility of securing the freedom of slaves, while the South was focused on states' rights and property rights, the latter of which they believed supported the continued ownership of slaves.

By morning news of the raid had spread and the Virginia Militia exchanged gunfire with Brown and his ragtag band of abolitionists. By the next day, Washington Marines commanded by Robert E. Lee joined the militia and demanded Brown's surrender. His counter-demands led the Marines to assault his position and take Brown into custody. He stood trial ten days later, was found guilty, and sentenced to death by hanging. His action had stirred the hearts of a nation.[vii] John Brown had lit a fuse that sparked rebellion in the South and anger in the North.

The raid at Harper's Ferry in 1859 and the upcoming elections lit the fuse on the powder keg of secession. The expansion of slavery into the west was a topic that became the debate among the candidates for President in 1860. In the North the people rallied behind an Illinois politician who spoke about the right of Congress to control the expansion of slavery into the territories. The South rallied around John C. Breckenridge as their salvation against the ever-growing anti-slavery movement. The election turned into a four-man battle for the Presidency, the viewpoints of which were as varied as the men running for office. This four-man race would be a large part of a change in American politics.

The four-man contest between Abraham Lincoln, John C. Breckinridge, John Bell, and Stephen A. Douglas was a heated and volatile occurrence. In the end Abraham Lincoln won the popular and electoral vote, with 180 electoral votes and almost forty percent of the popular vote.[viii] The election result was a catalyst for conflict. An anti-slavery President was to be sworn into the White House and the South was unhappy with the direction of the nation.

A wave of change was ready to sweep the Union. Its effect would be felt for years, decades, and generations to come. The tide was turning against the institution of slavery. With the election reflecting the division of the nation, the eventuality of Abraham Lincoln as President was a prospect that frustrated many and set the union on a course that would forever change the nation.

Chapter 2 – The Foundation Cracks

With the changing landscape, and each side of the slavery debate willing to shed blood for their cause, the nation sought to find a middle ground. Many were not open to discussion as each side stood its ground, pushing their beliefs to the west and seeking the government's intervention in the longtime debate. However, some sought to stand their ground and chose to make moves that would have ramifications for years to come.

South Carolina Leads Secession

Following Lincoln's election, the South began to grumble. Lincoln's platform was very much anti-slavery and clearly stated that "Government cannot endure permanently half slave, half free..."[ix] This statement by Lincoln prompted South Carolina to secede from the Union on December 20, 1860, a little more than a month after Lincoln had won the Presidency.

With the departure of one state, the fuse was lit for a full secession from the Union. South Carolina looked to be the example for the rest of the South. Slowly the wheels of changed moved in a direction feared by both the North and by the Union as a whole. A change was coming, but what that change would be was still unclear.

As Lincoln made his way towards Washington, he reiterated his stance and sought to let the people know that he was going to be standing for the Constitution and would uphold the current fugitive slave laws. The goal of the Republicans was to find a peaceful compromise to end slavery. With the secession of South Carolina, there was fear amongst many that there would be a resolution, but that it might not come peacefully.

Fort Moultrie

Following the secession of South Carolina, the Union sought to keep a hold on the defiant state. However, their forces were spread too thin. On December 26, 1860, Major Robert Anderson decided to leave the South Carolina installation at Fort Moultrie, and garrison his troops on an island off the coast of Charleston, South Carolina, named Fort Sumter. By doing this, he hoped to be able to more strongly defend against an attack by the militia of South Carolina. Anderson's abandonment of Fort Moultrie emboldened the South to take and claim the Fort for the Confederacy.[x]

With Anderson's army at Fort Sumter, the South had isolated the Union forces to a single island off the coast of South Carolina. A major change had occurred for the South. With the Union ostensibly on the run in the minds of the South, a clear psychological victory had been achieved. The South had now claimed a Union fort and built a military presence, essentially becoming a foreign power occupying the United States, something not seen in almost a hundred years.

The liberation of Fort Moultrie was not only a huge psychological victory for the South but a big blow to the Union, who wanted to maintain peace and find a way to keep war from coming to the Union. Fort Moultrie's abandonment by the Union epitomized the fear and abandonment felt by the South, sentiments onto which the Confederacy would latch. These strong emotions fueled the South's transformation into the Confederate States of America.

Confederate Constitution

On February 8, 1861, the delegates of the secession states met in Montgomery, Alabama, to adopt the Provisional Constitution of Confederate States of America. Jefferson Davis was chosen as their President and took the oath of office on February 18, 1861.[xi] This drastic separation and formation of an entirely new Republic at the back door of the Union was a slap in the face to Lincoln and the Union.

In his inaugural address Davis warned the North that this was a drastic shift in the state of the Union. He warned the North that the South just wanted to go its separate way and to be left alone. Lincoln also sought to keep peace, but he made it abundantly clear that the Union was more important than the wants of the Southern states. As Lincoln made ready to give his first inaugural address, many held their collective breath hoping that he would preach a peaceful solution rather than bellowing threats of war.

A Nation and a State Divided

In the northwest counties of Virginia, a rebellion was brewing. In this case, it was Unionists rising up against the Confederate powers in Richmond. On May 13, 1861, 425 delegates from northwest Virginia met with the intent of seceding from Virginia and becoming a new state under the laws and protection of the Union. Although fraught with questionable voting practices and other issues, the charter was ratified and the state of West Virginia was created.

Even though West Virginia was under the Union flag, it was teeming with Southern sympathizers. The northern panhandle delegates who developed the state charter wanted to put the capitol in Wheeling where there was more support for the Union. However, Southern loyalists from southern West Virginia didn't want their capitol to be that far north and devised a plan to move it further south.

When the time came to vote on the permanent capitol, legislators from the southern counties of the state started a smear campaign against Wheeling. They argued that the northern constituents didn't support the same values as the majority of the population in the southern portion of the state. Their argument was so convincing that Wheeling didn't even make the ballot and Charleston became the permanent capitol of the state.

The Presidents

The men who led both nations were two of the key players in the Civil War for very different reasons. Even though neither man raised arms on behalf of their nations, their decisions ended the lives of more than 600,000 soldiers. Both men came from somewhat humble backgrounds and yet reached the pinnacle of public service in their respective countries. One man would lead his nation to its demise, while the other would lead his country to its rebirth.

Jefferson Davis

Davis was born in Fairview, Kentucky on June 3, 1808. The youngest of ten children, Davis moved twice in his childhood years ending up in Louisiana via Mississippi. After his father's death at the age of 14, Davis' brother became his surrogate father and pushed him through his education. At the age of 16, Davis' brother got him an appointment at the United States Military Academy. After graduating in the bottom third of his class, and being court-martialed along with 30 percent of his classmates for spiking the Christmas eggnog, he was stationed at Fort Crawford, in the Michigan Territory.

In 1844, he won the election for his first political office representing Mississippi in the United States House of Representatives. When the Mexican-American War broke out, Davis resigned from the House and pulled together a regiment of volunteers from his district to fight in the conflict. Davis fought bravely in multiple battles in the war.

He was even dragged off the field of conflict after being shot in the foot during the Battle of Buena Vista.

After the war, Davis returned to Mississippi a hero. He was nominated by the governor to fill a vacancy in one of their senate seats and his appointment was ratified by the state congress in January 1848. He served in that capacity for five years until newly elected President Franklin Pierce picked Davis to be his Secretary of War. During his time in that office, he laid plans for the Transcontinental Railroad and increased the army's size and pay.

After Pierce lost re-election and Davis lost his position of Secretary of War, he won back his seat in the Senate for the state of Mississippi. During this stint as senator, tensions were rising between the North and the South. Heated debates and even violence on the floors of Congress eventually led to the inevitable succession of the state of Mississippi.

Once his home state seceded, Davis contacted the Governor to offer his services to Mississippi. He was made a general in the state's militia but was then nominated for President of the Confederate States of America. On February 19, 1861, Jefferson Davis was sworn in as the first and only holder the office of the fledgling country.

Abraham Lincoln

On February 12, 1809, the sixteenth President of the United States of America was born. In a small one-room log cabin in Hodgenville, Kentucky, Abraham Lincoln breathed air into his lungs for the first time. After many land title disputes in Kentucky, his father moved their family to Indiana due to lack of trust in the land management practices of the Kentucky government.

While living on the Indiana frontier, soon after his ninth birthday, Lincoln's mother died of milk sickness. His father remarried a widow with children of her own a year later. Lincoln became extremely fond of his father's new bride, eventually accepting her as his true mother. Frontier life did not suit young Lincoln. The typical chores bored the self-made scholar. He had more of proficiency in reading, writing, and composing poetry than he did operating a plow.

By the time he reached his teens, Lincoln had become more accustomed to the pioneer lifestyle. He became adept at swinging an ax and won many wrestling matches amongst local ruffians. However, another outbreak of milk sickness along the Ohio River scared the family enough to make them relocate once more. This time they headed further west, near Decatur, Illinois. After another failed attempt at homesteading by his father, Lincoln decided it was time to blaze his own trail.

Getting a job on a flatboat in New Salem, Illinois, his crew was tasked with transporting a load of goods via the Sangamon River to New Orleans, at the mouth of the Mississippi. As Lincoln unloaded the flatboat in New Orleans, he saw for the first time the brutal reality of slavery. Families being separated at auction, brutal fighting pits for entertainment and the rape of slave women were imprinted on his brain as he headed back home to Illinois, where he would spend the next six years.

During those six years, Lincoln failed in the mercantile business, became an officer in the militia during the Black Hawk Wars, and ran a failed campaign for local office. However, being an avid learner, Lincoln decided to begin studying law. He did not attend any schools; he just read as many law books he could find. He was admitted to the Illinois Bar in 1836, and he practiced law in Springfield, Illinois, until 1844. During his time in Springfield, he was also elected to the Illinois House of Representatives for four straight terms.

Lincoln's advancement to national politics happened in 1846 when he was elected to the United States House of Representatives as a member of the Whig party. After pledging to serve only one term as a representative, Lincoln's hopes of joining the new administration's cabinet were thwarted when they picked his political rival from

Illinois. Lincoln was resigned to practicing law again in Illinois after his hopes of staying in Washington were dashed.

Lincoln stayed away from the spotlight for the next few years until giving his opinion on the Bleeding Kansas incident. It was not until late October 1854 that he publicly denounced slavery in a speech in Peoria, Illinois. However, due to the Whig Party split over the slavery issue, Lincoln left in hopes of winning an Illinois senate seat as a Republican from the incumbent Democrat Stephen Douglas.

During the run for the Senate, Lincoln and Douglas partook in a series of seven debates that would become the base argument for not only the legality of slavery, but also the ethical legitimacy of the trade. Most considered Lincoln the winner of the debates and the Republicans won the majority of the popular vote. But, according to the laws at that time, the legislature picked the Senator. Since the majority of the state's legislature were Democrats, Stephen Douglas got the seat in spite of the voters' choice.

Even though Lincoln lost the Senate race, the campaign not only raised his profile in general, but also his popularity in the Republican Party. As 1860 and the next presidential election approached, Lincoln had become a frontrunner for the nomination. On May 18, 1860, Lincoln received the Republican nomination for president and began his rise to fame.

Lincoln's Inauguration

On March 4, 1861, Abraham Lincoln was sworn in as the sixteenth President of the United States.[xii] His speech during this swearing in had undercurrents of anger. He was sworn to defend the Union and he would do everything in his power to find a peaceful way to reunite a fractured Union. He used strong and stern language, but never directly threatened the newly-forming Confederacy. He desired peace and sought to find a solution to appease all sides.

When Lincoln stood to make his speech in 1861, he believed that there was still time to rally many in the South to the side of the

Union and encourage them to help reach a peaceful resolution, avoiding any further conflict. Through his mastery of words, Lincoln was a natural at the art of persuasion. By way of his many speeches along the campaign, as well as at his inauguration, he had stirred up respect, hope, and even anger. This inaugural address was intended to address all the concerns of both the North and the South as to what he and his administration hoped to accomplish. Although he knew that taking too strong a stance against slavery would provoke the South, he also knew that he had to stand firm regarding the laws of the land and the prevailing view of slavery in the Union.

"Apprehension seems to exist among the people of the Southern States that by the accession of a Republican Administration their property and their peace and personal security are to be endangered. There has never been any reasonable cause for such apprehension. Indeed, the most ample evidence to the contrary has all the while existed and been open to their inspection. It is found in nearly all the published speeches of him who now addresses you. I do but quote from one of those speeches when I declare that-- I have no purpose, directly or indirectly, to interfere with the institution of slavery in the States where it exists."[xiii]

Lincoln wanted to be clear that he was a supporter of the law the Constitution as well as states' rights. However, many in the South took his comments about the Fugitive Slave law as a statement of his intention to take things further. His goal was to convey his intention to enforce what was already on the law books and not needlessly burden the courts or the South with more laws. Lincoln had every intention of finding a way to abolish slavery. However he did not want that to come at the expense of war or unnecessary bloodshed.

"There is much controversy about the delivering up of fugitives from service or labor. The clause I now read is as plainly written in the Constitution as any other of its provisions: No person held to service or labor in one State, under the laws thereof, escaping into another, shall in consequence of the law or regulation therein be discharged from such service or labor, but shall be delivered up on claim of the party to whom such service or labor may be due."[xiv]

Lincoln did warn the South sternly that his full intention was to maintain the Union. He knew that in order to maintain peace he would have to warn them that the Constitution was law and that he intended to abide by it. It was meant to be a moment of clarity for the South; for them to see that by keeping the institution of slavery alive they were not abiding by the Constitution. With this statement about the Constitutionality of slavery, he urged the South to rethink their situation, to realize that they were not following the intention of the Constitution, and to amend their laws so they would reflect the supreme law of the land.

"A disruption of the Federal Union, heretofore only menaced, is now formidably attempted. I hold that in contemplation of universal law and of the Constitution the Union of these States is perpetual. Perpetuity is implied, if not expressed, in the fundamental law of all national governments. It is safe to assert that no government proper ever had a provision in its organic law for its own termination. Continue to execute all the express provisions of our National Constitution, and the Union will endure forever, it being impossible to destroy it except by some action not provided for in the instrument itself."[xv]

With the intention to enforce the Constitution, Lincoln fiercely warned the South that there would be no use of force unless they struck first. He intended to keep the Union from dissolving and would use all legal and military means to enforce the Constitution, the laws of the land, and the continued peace of the United States. He denounced the legal right of secession and wanted to end the notion before it took root in the South. The firm stance against any action to threaten or disrupt the Union was one that Lincoln did not take lightly. Many in the South saw this part of his speech as a direct threat against their freedom, as well as a condemnation of their desire to secede from the Union in order to maintain their way of life and free themselves from the rule of Lincoln and his perceived tyranny.

"But if destruction of the Union by one or by a part only of the States be lawfully possible, the Union is less perfect than before the Constitution, having lost the vital element of perpetuity. It follows from these views that no State upon its own mere motion can lawfully get out of the Union; that resolves, and ordinances to that effect are legally void, and that acts of violence within any State or States against the authority of the United States are insurrectionary or revolutionary, according to circumstances."[xvi]

Using even stronger words, the speech went on to state that the Union itself was the backbone of liberty, justice, and the supreme law of the land. Any attempt to destroy the Union would be an act of war, and the Union would do everything within its power and scope to keep itself intact and running as it had for all the years since its inception. The Union and the states within it were older than the Constitution, and the South was a necessary part of the Union. Lincoln knew that with division would come a great change to the face of America.

"I trust this will not be regarded as a menace, but only as the declared purpose of the Union that it will constitutionally defend and maintain itself. In doing this there needs to be no bloodshed or violence, and there shall be none unless it be forced upon the national authority. The power confided to me will be used to hold, occupy, and possess the property and places belonging to the Government and to collect the duties and imports; but beyond what may be necessary for these objects, there will be no invasion, no using of force against or among the people anywhere. Where hostility to the United States in any interior locality shall be so great and universal as to prevent competent resident citizens from holding the Federal offices, there will be no attempt to force obnoxious strangers among the people for that object. While the strict legal right may exist in the Government to enforce the exercise of these offices, the attempt to do so would be so irritating and so nearly impracticable withal that I deem it better to forego for the time the uses of such offices."[xvii]

Lincoln stood firm on his belief in the abolishment of slavery, which hit a nerve in the South since it was their main means of production. He pleaded for moral citizens to step forward and find a way to keep the Union together and to not let slavery be the issue that caused distrust and separation. He intended to use the Constitution to maintain the laws of the Union while also warning the South that he would use all resources at hand to maintain the Union. Again, many in the South felt threatened by Lincoln's statements and this further motivated them to try to blaze a trail away from Union and toward the formation of a nation within a nation.

"One section of our country believes slavery is right and ought to be extended, while the other believes it is wrong and ought not to be extended. This is the only substantial dispute. The fugitive- slave clause of the Constitution and the law for the suppression of the foreign slave trade are each as well enforced, perhaps, as any law can ever be in a community where the moral sense of the people imperfectly supports the law itself. The great body of the people abide by the dry legal obligation in both cases, and a few break over in each. This, I think, can not be perfectly cured, and it would be worse in both cases after the separation of the sections than before."[xviii]

Lincoln explained that secession and violence were not the proper ways to change the government, but that a constitutional amendment was the only acceptable method means of getting what they wanted. However, with a Republican majority, the South did not see that as a promising option. Lincoln knew that each state had the ability to generate such an amendment and bring it forward, but many sensed it would die in Congress, as the abolishment of slavery was in the conscience of the majority.

"This country, with its institutions, belongs to the people who inhabit it. Whenever they shall grow weary of the existing Government, they can exercise their constitutional right of amending it or their revolutionary right to dismember or overthrow it."[xix]

As religious as Lincoln was he also knew that Christian ideology was important in the South, and he pleaded with them to take a hard look at their spiritual teachings and see that what they were doing as slave owners would be frowned upon by God. Lincoln understood that the majority would have the final say and that the momentum against slavery would bring about a fair resolution.

"If the Almighty Ruler of Nations, with His eternal truth and justice, be on your side of the North, or on yours of the South, that truth and that justice will surely prevail by the judgment of this great tribunal of the American people."[xx]

With his threats leveled at the South, Lincoln urged them to take time and not be rash. Rushing in into secession or war would lead to irrevocable consequences, which would be detrimental to both the North and the South. The cautionary nature of Lincoln and his belief that anything could be resolved with words, and without bloodshed, gave him hope and was intended to encourage all people of the Union and the South to seek peace before further blood was shed.

"My countrymen, one and all, think calmly and well upon this whole subject. Nothing valuable can be lost by taking time. If there be an object to hurry any of you in hot haste to a step which you would never take deliberately, that object will be frustrated by taking time; but no good object can be frustrated by it."[xxi]

Lincoln also reiterated his oath to the Constitution as a solemn oath unto God and the Union. With this oath, he knew it would be on his shoulders to maintain the Union and follow the will of the people. The will of the people was strongly against slavery, but he needed to find a way to keep the Union together, hoping that peace could be maintained long enough for the South to see the error of their ways and come to their own conclusion about slavery.

"You have no oath registered in heaven to destroy the Government, while I shall have the most solemn one to "preserve, protect, and defend it. I am loath to close. We are not enemies, but friends. We must not be enemies. Though passion may have strained, it must not break our bonds of affection. The mystic chords of memory, stretching from every battlefield and patriot grave to every living heart and hearthstone all over this broad land, will yet swell the chorus of the Union, when again touched, as surely they will be, by the better angels of our nature."[xxii]

His words, however, were not taken lightly in the South and a growing tide of disdain for the North surged forth, especially in South Carolina. The following day, Lincoln received an urgent message from a letter from Major Anderson stationed at Fort Sumter, requesting aid and reinforcements for his position in Charleston Harbor. Lincoln, knowing that he was in a precarious situation, ordered a relief mission. He demanded that the navy only land supplies to the troops at Fort Sumter and that no soldiers or further reinforcements be landed at the island.[xxiii] He also demanded that no Confederate troops be engaged unless the Confederates interfered. Fort Sumter had become a prize for both the Union and the Confederacy. With this bold move Lincoln had alerted the Confederacy to the value of the small island, giving them a target on which to set their sights.

The Confederacy had become emboldened and felt that the rash movement by the Union was a sign of weakness. The South sought to assert its independence while hoping that their military victory would drive the Union from the Confederate states and leave them in peace. Lincoln was not so quick to give up. He sought to find a solution to the rebellion, even one that could lead to war: something he had wholeheartedly sought to avoid.

Chapter 3 – The First Shot

Separation through election was the first step towards a divided nation. With the secession of the Southern states and the formation of the Confederate States of America, the next logical step was a movement by either the Union or the Confederacy towards further division. Either the Union would leave the Confederate states alone, or one of them would draw the other into a war, which Lincoln still wanted desperately to avoid. Only time would tell which side would make the first move. Lincoln aspired to resolve the situation diplomatically, but Davis had no problem with conflict. Soon the two would have to come to terms with the reality of the situation.

Fort Sumter

Following Lincoln's Inauguration, the South began to move forward with further secessions. On April 10, 1861, the Confederate Secretary of War Leroy Pope Walker demanded Fort Sumter's immediate evacuation and threated to reduce it to rubble should they refuse. Major Beauregard had been awaiting a response from the Union and in the meantime had encircled Fort Sumter with artillery and had 6,000 men ready for battle.[xxiv]

On April 12, 1861, the South again attempted to secure a peaceful surrender from Major Anderson of the Union army. Major Anderson was warned that if he did not comply and surrender within an hour he would be fired upon.[xxv] The Union would not concede.

Near dawn, Lieutenant Farley of the Confederate army fired the first shot. His shot signaled the beginning of a change as the rest of the Confederate battery opened up on Fort Sumter. Within its walls, Major Anderson braced for a purely defensive battle as his small army of 10 officers, and 68 soldiers could not mount a realistic offense. He was waiting for reinforcements.

It was not until later in the day when the Union fired the first shot at a floating battery anchored near Fort Moultrie, the abandoned Union fortress. The bombardment of Fort Sumter increased as the Confederate army fired oven-heated cannon balls known as "hot shot" into the base burning the walls and setting exposed wood on fire[xxvi].

As the day went on, there was a glimmer of hope as Captain Fox and the steamer *Baltic* sailed into view. The hope was short-lived, as fear of sinking caused the Union ship to turn back to sea and abandon the men at Fort Sumter. As night progressed, rain aided the men in Fort Sumter at putting out fires and the Confederate army took a respite from constant bombardment.[xxvii]

By noon of April 13, 1861, the bombardment had increased, and Fort Sumter was burning. The Fort had ceased returning fire and the Confederacy saw victory approaching. By 7 p.m., Fort Sumter had agreed to surrender. Terms were set and the troops at Fort Sumter departed the base on April 14, marching out to a 100-gun salute put on by the Confederacy for their brave enemies.[xxviii] The Confederacy had fired the first shot of the war and had come away victorious. The Civil War had officially begun.

The South Rises

Following the news of the Confederate victory at Fort Sumter, military volunteers started flocking to state militias to aid their brothers in South Carolina. From Virginia to Texas the news of the Southern victory emboldened the previously sullen South. The North was stunned and outraged that the Union had become so divided and reduced to warfare in order to resolve differences. Both sides became concerned that what started as a largely political response could turn into an all-out war.

Both Lincoln and the newly elected Jefferson Davis wanted to avoid bloodshed. Davis understood the advantage the North had in factories, population, and transportation. The South had about a third of the ability of the North. The odds were not in their favor. Davis pleaded with Lincoln to leave the South be and to let bygones be bygones. However, he still asked for 100,000 volunteers to come forward to prepare for war.

Lincoln also acted swiftly and on April 15, 1861, he also issued an order for troops. Lincoln requested 75,000 volunteers for three months' service via executive order.[xxix] Five days later he ordered a naval blockade on all Southern ports.[xxx] Lincoln sought to keep peace through military superiority. With Congress on spring recess, Lincoln acted in what he saw as the best way to maintain order until Congress could reconvene and aid Lincoln in either ending the war or declaring it.

Knowing that he needed to rally support and get public opinion on his side he scheduled a special session of Congress on the Fourth of July.[xxxi] The South replied in kind and rallied other states to secession. Some states like Virginia were scheduled to vote on secession, however state militias took matters into their own hands. On April 18, a Virginia militia raided Harpers Ferry. The South bombarded the arsenal. To keep weapons from falling into confederate hands, the Union set fire to 15,000 weapons and retreated across the Potomac River to Maryland. When the South arrived to claim the fort, they found 5,000 rifles in useable condition and considered the battle a victory.[xxxii]

Riding high on the victory and Harpers Ferry, the Virginia militia raided The Gosport Naval Yard. Upon hearing about the attempted seizure, the commander of the shipyard ordered every ship possible to head to sea, and any that were not seaworthy to be burned and scuttled. Only three vessels made it to sea. The South once again gained a victory, seizing the U.S.S. Merrimack as well as over 1,000 naval guns which could be used to reinforce other fortifications throughout the South.[xxxiii]

The U.S.S Merrimack would become known as the C.S.S. Virginia and become a threat to the Union navy. With these small victories the South gained momentum and volunteers. More and more people headed to Virginia to get in on the action and to savor the triumph of what they believed was an already won war. The zeal of victory was so contagious that even Jefferson Davis moved his seat of power to Richmond, Virginia. The tide of change swept through the South as Tennessee, Arkansas, and North Carolina joined the Confederate States of America, making the division of North and South even greater than before. With this taste of victory, the South banded together into a full-fledged nation united against what they saw as a common enemy. While the North licked its wounds and wondered what the fate of this great nation would be Washington D.C. was concerned, as was Lincoln. First blood had been drawn and the Union was worried about its future.

Chapter 4 – Welcome to War

July 4 1861, brought a special session of Congress. President Lincoln took bold action asking for 400,000 men and 400 million dollars to put a stop to the Southern rebellion.[xxxiv] He argued that instead of waging war he sought to reunite North and South, bringing an end to the division of the Union. Lincoln also implemented suspension of the writ of habeas corpus on or near military lines, meaning that Southerners could be detained without bringing them before a court.

Strategy moved to the forefront of the Union leadership. The goal of Lincoln and the Union army was to stop the rebellion as quickly as possible. A prolonged war would further divide the nation and pull resources into needless bloodshed. The Union leaders agreed that if Richmond fell the leadership of the South would also fall and the war would end. The sentiment of "On to Richmond" echoed throughout the North.[xxxv]

Lincoln and the Union leadership agreed. The Union army moved into the Shenandoah Valley in early July. A Confederate army responded to this action by moving into a separate position in the same valley. For the first time in almost two hundred years, war would be waged on the American continent. This time it was brother against brother, citizen against citizen. The stakes of the war were larger than ever before. The Union itself was under threat, and any resulting division could and would have lasting consequences. War was at hand.

An Introduction of the Generals

So much lore surrounds the generals that participated in this war that it is sometimes hard to discern myth from fact when remembering the actions of these men. However, to try to understand where they came from and who they were when they commanded the armies that would determine the future of the United States, for this is essential to understanding the methods they used.

Ulysses S. Grant

Born Hiram Ulysses Grant on April 27, 1822, the future President of the United States of America thrived in the tannery of his strict Methodist father. He not only showed proficiency in the ability to tan animal hides, but also excelled in riding and training the very horses for which his father's leather provided harnesses, bridles, and saddles.

His father used a personal favor from a local politician to get his son admitted to West Point at the age of sixteen. On the entrance form, the politician mistakenly wrote his name as "Ulysses S. Grant" instead of his actual name Hiram. When he tried to change the mistake, he was informed they could not change the records, so the name stayed with him throughout his life.

After a lackluster career at West Point where he finished in the bottom half of his class, he got his first assignment. Even though one of his only accomplishments at the Academy was his horse-riding ability, he was not given cavalry duty. He was assigned to the 4th Infantry Regiment just outside of St. Louis, Missouri. He did not mind his new role, but he had a slight distaste for the military after his subpar performance at the academy. He was looking forward to the end of his four-year tour of duty so he could return to civilian life.

After demonstrating bravery and skill in the Mexican-American War, Grant returned to civilian existence, working in his father's leather shop until the first shots of the Civil War were fired at Fort

Sumter. President Lincoln called for 75,000 troops to end the Southern insurrection. Grant had a renewed sense of patriotism and volunteered. Due to his prior military experience, he began training the other volunteers while waiting for his official recommission into the United States Army.

Robert E. Lee

Born to the Governor of Virginia and his wife on January 19, 1807, Lee's life began with the air of aristocracy and privilege that was routinely granted to the owners of large plantations like his father. However, life turned sour quickly for young Lee as his father was forced into debtor's prison. Lee was himself consigned to West Point and a life in the military.

In an almost mirror image of the West Point career of Ulysses S. Grant, Lee excelled at the Army's highest level of education. He finished second in a class of 45 and received no demerits during his entire tenure at the prestigious learning institution. At the time, the two ranking officers at West Point were based in the Army Corps of Engineers, so the curriculum was primarily centered on studies relevant to the engineering field. Therefore, with the majority of his formal education based in engineering, Lee began his military career helping build forts in Georgia and Virginia. He even oversaw the construction of the harbor in St. Louis.

Like Grant, Lee saw his first military action during the Mexican-American War. Working as a reconnaissance officer, he received many citations for his work and bravery during the march to Mexico City. After the war, he reluctantly accepted the position of Superintendent of the Military Academy at West Point. He believed his skills could be put to better use than trying to improve the infrastructure and courses of the institution, but he completed his work with pride and efficiency.

Lee had to take a two-year hiatus from the military beginning in 1857 when his father-in-law passed away. Like his own father, Lee's father-in-law was a large plantation owner in Mississippi. Also like his father, he was horrible with money and his financial dealings were in disarray at the time of his death. After failed efforts to find someone to handle the estate for him, Lee had to go to Mississippi to execute the will himself.

In his late father-in-law's will, he wanted to have his slaves emancipated within five years of his death. The plantation was huge. It had sprawling acres of land that were maintained by the slaves that his father-in-law wanted freed. Along with the sprawling acreage, there were huge amounts of debt that his father-in-law had incurred while mismanaging his plantation. There was no way Lee could allow so much "property" of the plantation to be given away for nothing.

Upon his arrival, Lee was greeted by several slaves that had heard of their former owner's will and did not want to work on the plantation anymore. When confronted, the slaves told him they were as free as Lee was and ran from the plantation. Lee tracked them down and brought them to plantation justice. He ordered the overseer to punish the men with 50 lashes and the women with 20 lashes. The overseer would not whip the women, so Lee had the constable brought to finish the job. Lee returned to service after his hiatus and continued his career.

Lee's first taste of the Civil War was at one of its most pivotal points. During John Brown's raid of the Harpers Ferry arsenal, Lee was ordered to retake the facility. Upon arrival, Lee found that the Harpers Ferry garrison had surrounded Brown and his insurgents inside the building. After a brief battle, Lee captured Brown and put an end to his rebellion.

Lee had been stationed in Texas before that state seceded from the Union. Lee did not initially believe in the secession of the states and returned to Washington D.C. for another command. However, on April 20, 1861, Lee turned in his resignation letter to his commanders because he could not bring up arms against his home state of Virginia; he subsequently joined the Confederate Army.

William Tecumseh Sherman

Born on February 8, 1820, to a state Supreme Court justice and his wife in Lancaster, Ohio, Sherman was given a life of opportunity despite having to hurdle major obstacles early in life. When Sherman was nine years old, his father died suddenly and left no inheritance to his mother for which to raise him and his ten siblings. Luckily, a neighbor who was in the House of Representatives took on the job of raising young Sherman and introduced him to the proper channels in order to succeed in life.

When Sherman was 16, his benefactor was able to pull strings and get Sherman a spot as a cadet at the United States Military Academy at West Point. He excelled academically at West Point, but some of the military acumen that the army required was not to Sherman's liking. He did not see the need to always have a freshly pressed uniform, shoes shined to mirror-like perfection, or why one had to snap to attention and give the proper salute when required. He estimated that he collected at least 150 demerits per semester at the Academy, and he accumulated so many that it cost him his rank as one of the top five graduates in his class.

Upon graduation, Sherman was ordered to report to an artillery regiment in Florida. While there, he battled the Seminole Indian tribe for control of the peninsular state. After the Seminole uprising had been squashed, Sherman began an administrative role in the Army. He boarded a military vessel and sailed around Cape Horn on route to the unsettled western expanse of California.

While most of his class from West Point was busy fighting the Mexican-American War, Sherman began surveying and speculating just ahead of the gold rush that was soon to hit the state of California. He even surveyed and speculated in the area that would become the capitol of the state, Sacramento.

In 1853, the newly-married Sherman resigned his commission and began working with a Missouri-based banking firm in San Francisco. The stress of the business climate in the Bay Area was causing

Sherman to have bouts of anxiety, which ultimately impacted his health negatively. Later in life, he would say that it was easier to lead men into battle than to do business in San Francisco.

Sherman returned to the military life by becoming the superintendent of a military school in Louisiana that would later become Louisiana State University. However, as the list of states that left the Union grew, Sherman decided to go to Washington to try to regain his commission in the Army. During inauguration week, Sherman's plea regarding the lack of readiness of the Union Army failed to catch Lincoln's attention. In frustration, he took the job as president of a streetcar company in St. Louis.

That position lasted a few scant months before the first shots were fired over Fort Sumter. After his discussion with the President, Sherman was hesitant to rejoin the Union Army. However, his love of country finally won out and he accepted the commission on June 7, 1861.

Thomas "Stonewall" Jackson

Jackson was born on January 21, 1824, in what is now the state of West Virginia. The exact location is not certain, however. Both Clarksburg and Parkersburg claim to be the birthplace of this Civil War legend. As typhoid fever spread across the area, Jackson's father and sister both contracted and died from the disease. At the age of nine, his mother remarried and gave birth to a half-brother. However, his mother grew ill and died as well, leaving him and his sister orphans.

He and his sister moved to Jackson's Mill where he worked at his uncle's gristmill. He moved to Clarksburg for a time with an abusive Aunt, but that did not suit Jackson. A year later, he trudged back through the wilds to Jackson's Mill where he spent the next six years with his Uncle.

In 1842, Jackson was accepted into the United States Military Academy at West Point. Due to his unstable upbringing, he lacked the formal educational background that the other cadets had received in their childhood. However, the stubbornness and work ethic that he would become famous for began to shine through. Even after starting near the bottom of the class, he graduated 17th out of 59.

After graduation, Jackson joined an artillery regiment fighting in the Mexican-American War. His personality came to the forefront during the battles of the war. He disobeyed direct commands if he felt they were detrimental to his troops. He once refused to retreat when he was caught by a Mexican artillery regiment that had him outgunned. He felt they would be more vulnerable to the shelling if they pulled up and retreated, so he refused the direct order to do so. Jackson's instincts proved to be right. Because he did not retreat, the Mexican artillery focused on him while a brigade of United States infantrymen closed in on the Mexicans and forced their surrender.

In 1852, Jackson took on the role of educator by accepting the position of Artillery Instructor at the Virginia Military Institute. His lack of humor and hypochondria made him very unlikeable to the cadets that he taught. He had a habit of memorizing every lecture that he taught and any time a student had a question he would just repeat what he memorized.

After Virginia seceded in 1861, Jackson began drilling troops for the Army of Virginia. He was given command of a brigade of infantry based in Harpers Ferry. He was in command of this brigade when he received his now-famous nickname, "Stonewall."

During the First Battle of Bull Run, Union soldiers were about to break the ranks of the Rebels. The Confederates reveled when they saw Jackson standing like a stonewall against the northern aggressors.

First Battle of Bull Run

The Union intended to move towards Richmond, Virginia. Their movement was dependent on railroad for more troops and supplies. The route they needed to take was through the Shenandoah Valley, an agriculture hotbed for the South as well as the most natural route to Richmond. The Confederate army knew that if the Union took Manassas Junction they would have an easy way to funnel military power deeper into the South and the war would quickly turn in favor of the North. The valley was a strategic point for both sides moving to take each other's capitals.

Leading the Confederate army was General Beauregard who had become a hero at Fort Sumter for the South. He was outmanned and was low on supplies, but he was determined to stand his ground at Bull Run.

On July 18, 1861, the Union army of 35,000 soldiers moved into the valley. A brigade under the command of Brigadier General Daniel Tyler poured into the valley and was cut down by a waiting Confederate army. He was able to retreat, but not without loss. 19 men died and 64 were wounded or missing.[xxxvi]

The Union had to return and figure out a new strategy. Finally, on July 21, 1861, the Union army attacked at Bull Run. They met the South on the battlefield, and for a while, the Confederate army overwhelmed them at Matthew's Hill. As the South advanced, they were met by an overwhelming Union army that eventually used its numbers to crush the Confederates. As the day dragged on Southern reinforcements plugged the holes and began to rally back, even though they were still technically in retreat. The turning point came when the 33rd Virginia captured the batteries near Henry House Hill. The batteries became a crucial point, and for the next few hours, the two armies gained control only to lose it again. Late in the afternoon, the Union army fell apart, and troops began to retreat with the Confederate army in pursuit. xxxvii

The First Battle of Bull Run had become a Confederate victory, strengthening their resolve and rallying more Southerners to what they saw as a winning cause. By the end of the day the battle had taken its toll on both sides as the Union departed with 470 dead, 1,071 wounded, and 1,793 either captured or missing. The Confederate faired only a little better with 387 dead, 1,582 wounded, and 13 missing.xxxviii

Neither side had achieved an overwhelming victory, but the Confederate states saw it as a major blow to the Union. Each side had taken losses larger than they had envisioned. The South, while still winning, had suffered a heavy toll for holding Bull Run. They had to find a way to weaken the Union. The Union had to find a way to use their superior numbers to push back the South and move to Richmond. The North decided a blockade would weaken the Southern economy. The South saw the blockade as an opportunity. The emboldened Confederacy took their war to the sea.

Monitor vs. Merrimack

War again came to Virginia, this time on the coast. The United States Navy had put a blockade on the Southern ports cutting off over 3,00 miles of coastline from import and export. Knowing that the blockade would severely limit the ability of the South to get resources and export their goods, the Confederates took the scuttled frigate U.S.S Merrimack, which had been captured during the raid on Gosport Naval Yard, armored it, and turned it into the C.S.S. Virginia.xxxix

The South made use of the supplies they had along the coastline. To defend their ports, the Confederates used mines, which were explosive charges anchored along shipping channels They also devised torpedoes by taking explosives and attaching them to a long pole and attaching the pole to an unarmored vessel. They would then ram the enemy vessel with the torpedo, and the torpedo would explode, causing damage.

The Confederates attempted many raids like this with the C.S.S. Hunley being the most notable. On February 17, 1864, the C.S.S. Hunley a submersible powered by eight men, rammed the U.S.S. Housatonic and sunk it in port. While the blow was important, the entire crew of the Hunley perished in the act.[xl]

The Merrimack, now under Confederate control, took to raiding Union ships, destroying the U.S.S Congress and the U.S.S Cumberland before meeting the Union ironclad U.S.S. Monitor. The U.S.S. Monitor was dispatched to protect the frigate U.S.S. Minnesota from falling to the same fate of the other Union ships. The U.S.S Monitor was the Union's ironclad guardian. The meeting of iron giants was underway off the coast of Virginia.

On March 9, 1862, the two ironclads went to battle off the coast of Hampton Roads, Virginia, shooting at each other from as close as a few yards to as far as half a mile. The two ships circled each other for hours firing barrage after barrage of cannon fire trying to stop the other. For four hours the two ships pounded each other, looking for weak spots. Finally, the two ships agreed to call the battle a draw. While the battle of these formidable ironclads was considered a stalemate, the Union army had won a strategic victory, as they lost no other wooden ships to the deadly Merrimack. A psychological victory over the Confederate navy was huge[xli]

This battle would change how war at sea was waged. The lessons of the and the lessons of that clash had pushed the Union to turn on Southern coastal towns, shutting down trade and keeping Confederate troops on the defensive, thereby distracting them from moving further northward. This tactic by the Union allowed them to keep more troops under siege and away from larger battles which, with the Generals of the Confederate army leading them, could turn many future confrontations in the Confederacy's favor. The Union navy's ability to keep things at a standstill and bog down coastal troops was an advantage that cannot be overlooked.

Chapter 5 – Bloody Days

Battle of Shiloh

The worst of the war was soon to come. The armies of the Union, commanded by Ulysses S. Grant, and the armies of the South, commanded by Johnston and Beauregard, the hero of Sumter, met on April 6, 1862, in Shiloh, Tennessee. The two armies were camped only miles apart from each other in the valley with the Shiloh valley measuring 15 miles by 17 miles in the shape of a triangle.[xlii]

Grant was not confident about his strategy. He and his officers had not come up with a defensive plan and they had failed to put out scouts looking for impending attacks from the Confederate army. Johnston and Beauregard snuck up on the flank of the Union. The Confederates arose during the darkness of the morning, and volleys of artillery flew from the Confederate lines.

As the Union retreated, the Confederates looked to keep the pressure on. The resulting clash confused both Union and Confederate soldiers as they collided in the mid-morning hours. The Confederate army swept into the confused Union lines, and the latter were left attempting to create some sort of defensive measure.

Grant attempted to rally the troops. He pushed men into the weak spots of the Confederate line and prepared for prolonged action. The Confederates pushed forward, bombarding the Union lines. As they overran Union camps, the Confederate army began to falter. The

Confederate troops ceased moving forward and began to scavenge the Union camps. The Union pulled back troops to keep a tight line, inflicting heavy casualties on the attacking Confederate forces.

The Confederate army moved to flank the Union army. As they did so, the Confederate General Johnston was killed in battle. This concerned the Confederate troops, but Beauregard assumed command and moved the Confederate forces forward. By noon the Union army had retreated towards the Savannah River, leaving troops to protect an area called the Hornet's Nest. As the day continued the odds were against the Union soldiers at that position. They were called into retreat and despite attempting to flee, a group of 2,200 men was forced to surrender to the Confederate forces that evening.[xliii]

Grant fell back and created a line of soldiers known as "Grant's last line". Grant's line of 4,000 men and fifty guns readied themselves for the onslaught of the Confederate army. The Confederate forces pushed towards the Union position with 200 men, only to be cut down as they approached the line. As the sun fell the two armies retreated and set in for a long rainy night.[xliv]

During the night 25,000 fresh Union troops arrived to reinforce Grant's army[xlv]. The Union army prepared to push back the Confederate lines, and by 10 a.m., the full force of the Union was upon the Confederacy. The entire Union line erupted with fire from the soldiers' muskets as they marched towards the Confederate forces. By mid-afternoon, Beauregard saw the writing on the wall and called for a retreat of Confederate forces. The Confederate forces' losses were heavy from Shiloh, with 1,728 killed, 8,012 wounded and 955 missing, for a total loss of 10,694. Shiloh became the largest battle fought on American soil. The Union lost a considerable amount during the battle as well with 1,754 killed, 8,408 wounded, and 2,885 missing, with a total loss of 13,047 soldiers.[xlvi]

Shiloh damaged both sides psychologically, as the Confederates retreated and the Union headed further south. The loss took its mental toll as soldiers saw mounds of dead strewn across the battlefield where they marched. Grant had won a victory, but at a heavy cost.

The Seven Days Campaign

Outside of Richmond Virginia, General Lee of the Confederate army prepared for a Union advance. With an army of over 50,000, he prepared to face an advancing Union army of over 100,000.[xlvii] As he waited for the Union troops to arrive, Lee used his downtime wisely, procuring food and new uniforms for his troops. He stressed discipline and preached sobriety among his army.

Lee sent scouts to check on the approaching army under McClellan. He pulled Stonewall Jackson in and the two planned a full assault to begin on June 26. As he pushed his army forward, Stonewall Jackson and his forces arrived, supposedly to help push against the dug-in Union army. Instead, Jackson had his army set up camp and rest. The momentum gained early had come to a complete halt.[xlviii]

Lee still pushed forward and at Mechanicsville, he suffered heavy casualties. The Confederate army losses totaled 1,484 men killed or wounded while the Union only lost 361 soldiers.[xlix] During the night McClellan bolstered his flank knowing that Stonewall Jackson's army would be moving in the following morning.

On June 27, Lee pushed towards the established Union encampments, only to find them emptied during the night. The Confederate forces chased the Union to Gaines' Mill where they proceeded to rush forces at the Union line. The Union line held and kept the advancing Confederate army at bay. Soon Jackson's army arrived and together they pushed into the Union line breaking it apart. The Union line began to crumble and the Confederate Generals could see a glimmer of victory.

In full retreat, the Union army under McClellan abandoned their entrenchments outside Richmond and moved across the river. Lee, sensing something afoot, rallied his own troops and Jackson's to attack the front and rear of the Union army.

On the June 29, the two armies moved to converge on the fleeing Union forces. However, Jackson's army ran into trouble at Grapevine Bridge and spent the day rebuilding it in order to cross. The Union army snaked further away, and the 10-mile line stretched so far apart that they were vulnerable to Confederate attack. Jackson's army could come from the north and Lee's could come from the west, rendering the Union army defenseless. The easy victory was not to be. Instead of Jackson heading to cut off the Union from the North, he finished his bridge building and then proceeded to round up Union stragglers. A huge opportunity was squandered.[l]

Lee continued to move his army forward. He took his troops towards Glendale and sought to take out a Union brigade guarding a supply train. With 18,000 men he attacked the Union brigade, and as he pressed forward, the Union mounted a counterattack, stopping the Confederate advance. As night approached, the fighting between the two armies ceased and the day's losses were counted with Lee and the Confederates losing 3,300 to the Union's 2,853.[li]

The following day Lee pushed south of Glendale towards Malvern Hill. Atop the hill were 250 Union artillery, which Lee bombarded for hours. As he wore down the barrage, he pushed his army forward towards the Union troops at Malvern Hill. Confederate troops climbed an 800-yard slope as Union cannons tore holes in the Confederate waves that surged forward. By evening, the Seven Days Battle was over. The Confederates had stopped the Union push to Richmond and the Union had taken what was left of their army to retreat back north.[lii]

The campaign cost both sides many more lives and did nothing but invigorate the Confederates' narrative that they could defeat the

Union. At the end of the campaign, the Union had suffered 15,849 lost soldiers while the Confederacy had taken a huge blow with the loss of 20,141 soldiers.[liii]

Second Battle of Bull Run

In August 1862, The Union commander again decided to take Manassas at Bull Run. With a new Army of Virginia and the Army of The Potomac. With the Confederacy having pushed back the Union during the Seven Days Campaign the Union needed a victory. They had an opportunity as the army of General Lee was surrounded on one side by McClellan's army with the new Union commander John Pope bringing his army to bear.

Lee used strategy to move his army towards Pope's and separate his forces, sending half with Stonewall Jackson and leaving half behind to protect Richmond, the prized capital of the Confederacy. Jackson and his army advanced towards Pope's and pushed them back to Cedar Mountain, slowing their movement and forcing them to wait for McClellan to come to reinforce Pope's army. Knowing that McClellan was on his way, Lee again split his forces and attacked Pope's dwindling army.

By August 26, the Confederate army had cut off Pope's supply line from Washington, seizing and destroying a Union supply depot at Manassas Junction, thereby leaving the Union stuck back at Bull Run. Lee reunited his army with Jackson's and they met Pope on the battlefield of Bull Run once again. Jackson and his army dug into the shelter of an unfinished railroad station, and the two lines held because Pope could not coordinate his attacks.[liv]

On August 30, 1862, the Union army pushed back against Jackson's troops, but again the Confederate line held. As the day went on, Confederate reinforcements arrived and drove the Union army back to Henry Hill, where the Confederates had made their final stand almost a year earlier. The Union held the hill overnight, and under cover of darkness, Pope sent most of his army in retreat.

In the morning the Union was all but gone, and Jackson pushed them back out of the valley and into Washington, where they retreated behind the defenses of the Union capital. The Second Battle of Bull Run was a success for the Confederates. The Union suffered a loss of 14,462 men while the Confederates lost only 9,474.[lv]

With the Union army pushed back into Washington, General Lee had no way to strike. The fortifications around the Union capital were too strong, and the Union had more troops, giving them at least a two-to-one advantage over the Confederacy. Knowing that this could be the push the Confederacy needed to win the war Lee decided to push north into Maryland.[lvi]

The Push North

As Lee pushed north, he received a reinforcement of 20,000 fresh soldiers. By the time Lee made it to Maryland, his army numbered 50,000.[lvii] Lee then split his army into four elements and sent them to Harpers Ferry, the Potomac, and the Shenandoah to reinforce the supply lines. The race to the North was on.

The North now had to confront the Confederate threat pushing into Maryland. With Lee moving north, they had no way to know his plans. However, on September 13, 1862, two Union soldiers found three wrapped cigars on the ground.[lviii] Wrapped around the cigars were the orders Lee had sent to his commanders for the four-way split. The orders were given to McClellan, and the Union now had an ace up their sleeve.

McClellan pushed to overtake Lee's split army and to crush Lee at Sharpsburg, Virginia, meeting him on the grounds near Antietam Creek. The move by McClellan was one that would be a game changer. Rather than being on the defense, the Union sought to push the Confederates back into the South and maintain a barrier between them and Washington. Any incursions above Virginia would put the Union in a risky position.

Antietam

On September 17, the Union army approached Lee's and Jackson's armies at Antietam. As cannons opened up with volleys from both sides, the Union army pushed through the field and into a cornfield filled with the ranks of the Confederacy. Inside the stalks of corn, soldiers met in a blinding and fierce fight that went on throughout the morning.[lix]

One brigade of Confederate soldiers suffered a fifty percent casualty rate from the cornfield. The Union and Confederacy fought in the cornfield at point-blank range pushing each other back fifteen times covering the cornstalks in blood.[lx]

The Federals pushed through the field and into the pike, which the Confederate army had reinforced. As the Union pushed into the Confederate line, they were greeted by a waiting Georgia unit who fired on them as they approached. The Union kept pushing forward and the Confederates were falling back.

Jackson's army had been eating food and was resting in preparation for a later battle. However the approaching Union army roused them and angered them by interrupting their meal, the first they had gotten in days. The 2,300-man division rushed the Union line and pushed them back to the cornfield, saving the morning for the Confederates.[lxi]

The Confederate division was met by fresh Union troops who drove them back across the pike and into the woods. They suffered high casualties, and the Union pushed past their previous position and fought across the valley. By 9 a.m. the casualties on both sides had become staggering, with over 8,000 mean dead on both sides.[lxii]

As the Union army pushed forward, they were squeezed perilously close to one another. The 15th Massachusetts were so crowded that they ended up taking fire from the Union as well as the Confederate army, causing them to lose 344 men from both sides of fire.[lxiii]

The Confederate army fell back to a hill and a trench that they had bolstered with rifles in anticipation of the Union charge. The army lay in wait as the Union soldiers came over a crest only 100 yards away. As they started down the slope, the Confederate rifle trench opened up on them taking out the entire front line of the Union army. More and more Union soldiers poured into the line and were cut down giving the area the nickname Bloody Lane.

The Confederates, who were being pursued by the Union army, retreated into an orchard with the enemy at their heels. The Union chased them down and cut down more of the Confederate troops.

As the day progressed, the Union moved across the bridge at Sharpsburg, pushing the Confederates back. Lee had sent for reinforcements, and they were marching from Harper's Ferry to repel the advancing Union. As the Union army surged forward their lines had become weak.

The army arriving from Harpers Ferry advanced on them and cut into a gap in the Union line, mowing their soldiers quickly. Within minutes of the arrival of the Confederates from Harper's Ferry, the Union was pushed back through the cornfield, losing much of the ground they had won earlier in the day. The Union had fallen back, and the battle of Antietam was over. The loss of life on both sides was overwhelming. The union had 2,108 killed, 9,549 wounded, and 753 missing, for a total of 12,410 lost in the battle. The Confederates fared only slightly better with 1,546 dead, 7,752 wounded, and 1,018 missing.[lxiv]

With heavy losses on both sides, each withdrew to lick their wounds. The Union stayed outside Sharpsburg, but they had lost all the ground they had gained. Lee and the Confederates retreated across the river and back into Virginia. The war had arrived at a stalemate.

Chapter 6 – Proclaiming Freedom

Preliminary Emancipation

On September 12, only five days after Antietam, President Lincoln had a cabinet meeting. He had presented them with the first draft of the Emancipation Proclamation in July of 1862. Before the Battle of Antietam, Lincoln had made a promise to "myself and to my Maker" that should the Confederacy be pushed out of Maryland, he would issue the proclamation.[lxv] Following Lee's retreat back into Virginia, Lincoln planned to honor his promise.

On September 22, 1862, Lincoln issued the preliminary version of The Emancipation Proclamation. By issuing such a document, even preliminarily, he knew that he could take away some of the South's strength by providing an incentive for slaves to escape. This would provide a distraction and weaken the economic stability of the Confederacy. Without slaves for labor and with its men fighting, the Southern economy would be weakened.

Lincoln united the Republican Party to push for the complete abolishment of slavery and to stave off any military interference on the part of England or France. The Emancipation was a cut at the South just as they were gaining the upper hand. As he had stated in his first inaugural address, it was to be the will of the people and the Constitution that guided Lincoln's decision-making. Lincoln had hoped that the Confederates would come to their senses and abandon what he considered a lost cause. With the Emancipation Proclamation, the will of the people of the Union and the Constitution were thrust upon the Confederates. Whether or not they would end the war and return to the Union was entirely their choice.

Fredericksburg

Two months after Antietam, the Union and Confederates were in a different world. The Union had lost McClellan, and General Burnside had picked up leadership of the Union army. Lee and the Confederate army had reorganized and resupplied his army, separated them into two corps, and put them under the command of Jackson and Longstreet. Lee was using his leadership assets as much as his army to push back the Union.

By November, the Union had once again decided they needed to capture Richmond and put an end to the war. Burnside had decided that he would move towards Virginia and trick Lee into thinking he was going to take Gordonsville, and then at the last moment strike at Fredericksburg. Burnside intended for the strike to be fast and unexpected.

The plan to ferry supplies and troops via steamer faltered and Burnside was delayed in setting the attack. The delay allowed Lee to reinforce Fredericksburg and by the end of December, Lee's entire army of 85,000 was defending the Fredericksburg area.[lxvi]

Having delayed long enough, Burnside called upon gunboats to support the attack. However, as they approached, Confederate artillery pushed them back downstream and out of their supporting capacity. On December 11, the Union was set to invade Fredericksburg, and as they crossed the Rappahannock River in the early morning hours, they were met with fire from Confederate sharpshooters on the bank.

The Union artillery attempted to reinforce the troops crossing the river and to protect engineers who were trying to form a crossing. After an hour the artillery subsided, and the engineers went back to work again, only to be fired upon once more by Confederate sharpshooters. With the engineers pinned down and the army unable to move, the Union army brought forth 100 guns and fired 5,000 rounds into Fredericksburg.[lxvii] This did not deter the sharpshooters on the bank, and eventually, the Union was forced to launch pontoons of infantry across the river to claim the banks and remove the threat. As they crossed, they too were met with heavy fire. Once they reached the other side they moved out and cleared the bridges and banks, enabling the rest of the army to move forward. With this small victory, the Union army was able to push into Fredericksburg, and the Confederates were forced into retreat.

The Union spent the following day moving across the river without obstruction and looting the town of Fredericksburg. The Confederates under the command of Lee moved into a defensive position, lining up across the railroad tracks outside Fredericksburg. The Confederates had a strong defensive line except for a small wooded area between two bridges the Union army had to cross.

On December 13, under the cover of a morning mist, the Union pushed west and south into the waiting Confederate army. As the fog lifted, the shine of thousands of Confederate bayonets shone across the plains. The Union was shot at as they were crossing the plains and stalled in moving forward. Once the Union regrouped, they moved ahead, only to be bombarded by Confederate artillery ripping apart their ranks.

The Union moved through the unprotected wooded gap and into the Confederate lines. The confusion caused the Confederates to not fire upon the advancing Union soldiers, who then slaughtered the Southerners as they fell upon them. The confusion led the Union to break the Confederate line. Soon the Confederates flanked and attempted to push back the oncoming wave of Union soldiers, only to falter as they ran out of ammunition and other units fell back leaving the front lines unsupported. As both armies retreated to regroup, the casualties of the day mounted. The Union had lost 4,830 men, while the Confederates under the command of Jackson lost 3,415.[lxviii]

On the other side of Fredericksburg, more fighting occurred with Lee's troops holding Marye's Heights outside the city. The Confederates had taken a position behind a four-foot high stone wall enabling them to fire at oncoming Union troops with little to no exposure to return fire. The line was 2,000 strong with reinforcements just beyond the ridge of over 7,000 Confederate troops.[lxix] Artillery supported the Confederates at Marye's Heights and when the Union was forced to make a march out of the city and into an open plain, they would be assaulted as they trudged up a muddy bluff.

The Union was decimated by artillery as soon as they emerged onto the plains, yet they pushed forward towards the bluff. As they reached the last 125 yards of their march, the Confederates behind the wall opened up with volley after volley of rifle fire killing hundreds of Union soldiers.[lxx] Still, they pressed on, and some even made it up the bluff, pausing to fire back on the Confederate position and then falling back to reload.

The Union pushed on and was met with gunfire from the ridge. Not one Union soldier made it to the stone wall, and the Union suffered crushing losses. The Union army had 1,284 dead, 9,600 wounded, and 1,769 missing. The Confederates had 595 killed, 4,061 injured, and 1,769 missing.[lxxi] The Union was forced back and lost its momentum towards capturing Richmond.

Emancipation Proclamation

After the issuance of the preliminary Emancipation Proclamation, the Confederacy was offered the opportunity to end the war by the end of 1862. But, the offer was rejected.[lxxii] So, Lincoln moved to make the Emancipation Proclamation official. On January 1, 1863, Lincoln put the Emancipation Proclamation into effect. The proclamation made the war with the South not just a struggle to reunite the Union, but also a civil rights war for black liberation.

With the war at a stalemate and the Union needing a victory, Lincoln knew that by issuing the proclamation the South would have to deal with slave rebellions and insurrections. Abolitionists lauded Lincoln's daring move, and Jefferson Davis of the Confederate States condemned it.

The Union now began to recruit black soldiers and to create black units that would assist in freeing slaves in the Southern states. This push by Lincoln gave the Union a psychological, and eventually military, win as black recruits flocked to the Union army. By the end of 1865, the Union army had more than 180,000 black troops.[lxxiii]

While the Emancipation Proclamation did not end slavery, it did lead to freeing and arming slaves who rose up in aid of the Union. Foreign armies who may have once supported the Confederate states backed away, not wanting to be any part of a war that was now intended to stop slavery. The Emancipation Proclamation made the Confederate states reevaluate their position and contemplate the future of the war. With this new threat to their way of life, many wondered how the Confederacy would respond.

Impressment and Military Draft

As the war crept on, the South faced a shortage of supplies. With the Union blockading its ports, and the loss of slaves due to the Emancipation Proclamation, the Confederate states were forced to issue an impressment law which gave army officers the right to take any private property that would aid them in fighting the war. While this was already a common occurrence, this verbalized threat by the Confederate government caused many to worry about the future of the war and to question the legality and implications of such movements.

State governors issued officers to seize cattle, clothing, food, horses, iron, slaves, and even free men for the service of the Confederacy.

The taking of such goods usually was at a total loss for the property owner. In addition, the Confederacy issued a ten percent "tax in kind" on farm produce, fomenting further Southern anger against the government.[lxxiv]

While the Union also had such an act in place it was rarely used, and since the Union had a strong economy, it enabled them to use such acts sparingly. The Confederacy, however, was running ragged. Its currency was rapidly inflating, and the costs of goods and services were being repaid at an outdated rate rather than at a competitive one. The deterioration of the Confederate economy was adding another burden to the already stressed Southern states.

The Union however had bigger issues as they instituted a military draft. The draft required every man to serve in the army unless he could either furnish a substitute or pay the government three hundred dollars. These provisions in the draft law lead to many who were poor or unable to find a surrogate to be thrust into battle. Many of these people were immigrants and working-class folks who in July of 1863, after the names of draftees were published in the newspaper, marched through the streets, resulting in riots, property damage, and lynching. The Union army was sent in with soldiers straight from the front lines of the war. Sadly, when they arrived, they had little sympathy for the protesters and opened fire on the mob. This killed hundreds but ended the riots.[lxxv]

Chapter 7 – The War Looks Grim

The Union and Confederacy were both hurt as the war dragged into yet another year. In Mississippi, the Union led a raid which further upset the balance in the South. For 16 days, Colonel Benjamin Grierson led Union cavalry units from Tennessee to Louisiana, killing over 100 Confederate soldiers, freeing 500 Union troops, and destroying about 60 miles of railroad as well as 3,000 arms stored by the Confederates.[lxxvi]

The use of such guerilla tactics was intended to cause the Confederacy to divert its forces in pursuit of the Union cavalry, rather than pushing north. By drawing the forces away from the front and towards a smaller and quicker enemy, many of the resources were also redirected away from the front lines of the Confederate army. Grierson and his cavalry were a strategic move that gave the Union a much-needed edge.

Chancellorsville

Following winter quartering by both the Union and Confederate armies, the war was back on in May of 1863. Outside Fredericksburg, both armies had lingered following their December 1862 clash. The much-needed rest and recuperation experienced by both the Union and the Confederates were apparent.

The Union decided to move onto Chancellorsville and marched there without resistance. On May 2, Stonewall Jackson surprised the Union army from the west while Lee took his other forces and attacked from the south. Jackson and his 26,000 troops, who had found the Union troops napping and relaxing, caught the Union off guard. The Confederates fell upon the Union army and overran them easily.[lxxvii]

While some of the soldiers returned fire, other men scattered and ran from the rush of oncoming Confederate soldiers. The Union attempted to form a defense and stop the rush of Confederate troops. As night fell, Jackson pulled his line back and replaced his exhausted troops so he could attempt a night attack. Jackson rode out to scout the land himself as he returned from his reconnaissance of the Union lines, he was mistaken for a Union troop and shot by his own men. He was taken from the battlefield, his left arm was amputated, and was left to rest in the hope that he would recover.[lxxviii]

The Union spent the evening after the raid by Jackson's army reorganizing and preparing for a further assault. The Union troops made a loop around Chancellorsville, building up their fortifications the best they could. More troops poured in to reinforce the beleaguered Union army, swelling their ranks to 76,000 men.[lxxix]

The following day, with Jeb Stuart now in their command, Jackson's troops went to battle with the larger Union army. The Confederate troops came from all sides as the Union repelled wave after wave, pushing them back and forcing them to readjust their approach. By the end of the day both armies were exhausted and could no longer fight.

General Lee took full command on May 4 and hoped to push the army of the Union back both north and east. The two-attack approach of the Union had strained Lee's forces and supplies. Although the Union lost 17,287 soldiers, the Confederates had lost 12,764 as well as the ability to sustain any further heavy personnel and supply losses.[lxxx] The Confederacy was also about to suffer a misfortune that would be felt all across the South. On May 10 Jackson had succumbed to his wound and died in a field hospital outside Chancellorsville.[lxxxi] The Confederacy had suffered a massive blow to its leadership.

Gettysburg

Only months later would the Confederates resume their push north. This time the battlefield would be in Union territory, far north of Washington but within striking distance of it. The battlefield was Gettysburg, Pennsylvania. On July 1, 1863, Lee and his army arrived in Pennsylvania looking for another strategy to make their way into Maryland and neighboring Washington.[lxxxii]

In desperation, the Confederates saw Gettysburg as a path they could take to end the war. The first shot at Gettysburg was via a sentry responding to Confederate cavalry. The Union had men on the high ground waiting for an assault on Gettysburg. The Confederates assaulted the ridge and were pushed back. They saw the high ground as a necessary hold to win the battle.

As charge after charge pushed the Union line tighter and caused casualties, the Confederate army also suffered heavy losses, tearing apart their army and making each successive charge weaker and weaker. By July 3rd the Confederacy was at the end of their rope. With little land gained and many lives lost, they need something big to change the tide.

On July 3, Lee knew he needed to do something rash. Lee turned 150 guns and 15,000 men towards Cemetery Ridge, committing a frontal assault. Lead by Pickett's division this event would become known as Pickett's Charge. Beginning at 1 p.m., Lee had 150 guns bombard the Union line for two hours. The Confederate army had to march over open terrain to finish the final assault. As they rushed the Union positions, 80 guns blasted them apart. While Union soldiers hiding behind a stone wall opened up on the rest of the army, cutting them down where they stand by the end of the charge only 100 men reach the wall only to be called to retreat. The Battle of Gettysburg results in the single biggest defeat for the Confederacy.[lxxxiii]

Gettysburg saw over 160,000 soldiers engaging in a battle over three days. The Union had mustered 88,000 to the Confederates 75,000.[lxxxiv] By the end of the battle more than 28,000 Confederate soldiers were killed, injured, or lost while the Union suffered 23,049 losses.[lxxxv] Between the two sides, the dead at Gettysburg numbered over 6,000. Lee was forced to retreat to Virginia and out of Union territory.

Chapter 8 – Turning the Tide

As the fighting continues, each victory meant more than the last. The Union had the ability to keep the war going while every loss the Confederates took was a bigger blow to their cause and their war chest. Both sides had endured a war longer than they could have imagined. Lincoln had thought the rebellion would be crushed within a year and Davis had assumed that the Union would give up and let the Confederate States exist freely. Neither wanted to give up and lose the nations they had sworn to serve.

Vicksburg

Following the loss at Gettysburg, the Confederacy was growing weak. The Union had claimed several other victories securing New Orleans and Memphis from out of Confederate control, leaving Vicksburg as the last link between the two halves of the Confederate states.

General Ulysses S. Grant had the city under siege since May 18 of 1863.[lxxxvi] Having attempted to take the city two times, the Union had suffered massive casualties at the hands of the reinforced, and heavily fortified, Confederate army in Vicksburg. Grant had attempted frontal assaults, sea batteries, and bombardment. Finally, after learning of Lee's army arriving at Gettysburg, Grant pushed to find a way to take Vicksburg.

Having detonated a mine under the fortifications of the city, the Union was trying to force their way under and into the settlement. The city was starving; the people had begun running low on meat, salt, and even water. With Grant knocking at the door, the Confederacy was forced to find a way to end the siege at Vicksburg.

On July 3, 1863, the same day as Lee's defeat at Gettysburg, the leader of the troops at Vicksburg, General John C. Pemberton, sent a message of truce to Grant. The two met to set terms, and Grant asked for an unconditional surrender. Pemberton was willing to capitulate. Grant, however, rethought the situation and offered Pemberton and the Confederate troops parole. All the Confederate soldiers would be released after signing an oath to not fight again until all Union captives were free.[lxxxvii]

By midnight Pemberton had accepted Grant's terms and the siege of Vicksburg had ended after 48 long days. The siege had taken a huge toll on each army; so much so that they had comforted each other after the siege's end. The humanity of war had become more apparent to both sides. Many wondered how much longer the war could continue, how much longer citizen could fight against citizen.

Following the announcement of the fall of Vicksburg, one final holdout on the Mississippi at Port Hudson surrendered the garrison to the Union navy on July 9, 1863.[lxxxviii] The South was slowly falling. The mighty Mississippi had fallen to the Union and the Confederates had lost a vital passage for troops and trade.

Battle of Chickamauga

Tennessee was still a contested area or the Confederate army. They had held several areas around Chattanooga and were attempting to repel the Union from the state. On September 18, 1863, General Rosecrans and his army of 62,000 Union soldiers pushed to cut off the Confederate army and keep them from assaulting the Union army heading to Chattanooga. With 65,000 men the Confederate General Braxton Bragg met at Chickamauga Creek.[lxxxix]

The two armies clashed on September 19, with both suffering heavy losses and retiring at the end of the day without either making much advancement. During the night, however, the Union dug trenches and prepared for a Confederate assault. The following day the Confederate army rushed the Union defensive positions and forced them to plug gaps caused by the assault. As they were doing this, a second Confederate assault pushed the Union army back to a wooded ridge where they took a last stand while the bulk of the Union army retreated to Chattanooga. While this was a victory for the South, it did not turn the tide in their favor since they still suffered a loss of 18,454 soldiers versus the Union's somewhat smaller loss of 16,179.[xc]

The Union had retreated to the safety of Chattanooga, and the Confederates had only won a small win. Each victory, however, emboldened Davis and the Confederate leadership. Though their resources dwindled and their safety in Richmond was intermittently in peril, they still saw their cause as a just one. Lincoln too sought to state his dedication to the cause and soon used the battlefield at Gettysburg to restate his desire for an end to the war and a reunited Union.

Gettysburg Address

As the Union army picked up steam, pushing Lee and the Confederates out of the North while taking over New Orleans, Mississippi, and Tennessee, Lincoln decided that Gettysburg would be a perfect place to dedicate to a speech to restoring the Union.

On November 19, 1863, upon Lincoln's arrival at Gettysburg, ceremonies began with music, prayers, a two-hour speech by Edward Everett of Massachusetts followed by a hymn, and then a 272-word address known today as the Gettysburg Address.[xci]

Lincoln stood in front of a crowd of 10,00 and spoke slowly and loudly so all could hear. Lincoln proclaimed:

"Fourscore and seven years ago our fathers brought forth, on this continent, a new nation, conceived in liberty, and dedicated to the proposition that all men are created equal. Now we are engaged in a great civil war, testing whether that nation, or any nation so conceived, and so dedicated, can long endure. We are met on a great battle-field of that war. We have come to dedicate a portion of that field, as a final resting-place for those who here gave their lives, that that nation might live. It is altogether fitting and proper that we should do this. But, in a larger sense, we cannot dedicate, we cannot consecrate—we cannot hallow—this ground. The brave men, living and dead, who struggled here, have consecrated it far above our poor power to add or detract. The world will little note, nor long remember what we say here, but it can never forget what they did here. It is for us the living, rather, to be dedicated here to the unfinished work which they who fought here have thus far so nobly advanced. It is rather for us to be here dedicated to the great task remaining before us—that from these honored dead we take increased devotion to that cause for which they here gave the last full measure of devotion—that we here highly resolve that these dead shall not have died in vain—that this nation, under God, shall have a new birth of freedom, and that government of the people, by the people, for the people, shall not perish from the earth."[xcii]

The speech renewed the call for an end to the war and for the Union and the Confederacy to reunite. In front of a crowd and a free press Lincoln hoped his words would spread to the Confederate states and fall on the ears of Jefferson Davis, awaking in him the realization that the war could not be sustained. With more losses at Gettysburg than either side could handle, Lincoln hoped his speech would be an olive branch to the Confederates. He hoped that things would soon change. 1864 was indeed to be the year that the war changed.

Battle of Wilderness

On May 4, 1864, the Union entered Wilderness, Virginia. The Union army marched to take Wilderness and was cut off by Lee's troops at

Orange Turnpike. The two armies clashed, and a battle was fought through dense brush and foliage.

The two armies fought for three days with each pushing the other back. Confederate reinforcements arrived on May 6, and the battle raged on into the night. The battle was so tough that fires started in the brush, causing the armies to take time to stop the fires and remove the injured in order to prevent them from being burned to death.

While the battle was hard-fought, eventually the two armies ended with a draw. However, Grant considered it a victory for the Union as he and his army continued south further into Virginia.

The bloodshed at Wilderness was devastating for both sides; however, the Union took the brunt of the loss. The Union lost 1,766 soldiers compared to the Confederates' 7,500.[xciii] While Grant claimed victory, he paid a heavy toll at Wilderness.

Siege of Petersburg

In June of 1864, The Union once again pushed to take Richmond, Virginia. They needed to end the war. The strain on both the Union and the Confederacy was becoming unbearable. Hundreds of thousands of men had died for both sides, and the country was torn apart.

The Union pushed into Virginia and to Petersburg. Petersburg was the key to the railroad network that was keeping Lee and the Confederate army alive. Grant decided that if they could cut off supplies, they could shut down the Confederate army and move on to Richmond. Petersburg was heavily defended with artillery covering all the lines of fire and a network of trenches around the city. The Confederates had fortified the city against the oncoming Union army.

On June 18, 1864, Lee and his army met the Union army outside Petersburg and fought for four days, costing the Union 10,000 troops.[xciv] The small skirmishes continued on and off for the next three weeks with neither gaining ground. Thus began the siege of Petersburg.

Though the two armies sat only hundreds of yards apart, the Union had been given a golden opportunity. Soldiers from Pennsylvania who were former miners were only 130 yards from the Confederate line.[xcv] The Union formed a plan to dig under the Confederate defenses, blow a hole in it, and breach Petersburg claiming the city.

The miners dug 40 feet a day around the clock to move 510.8 feet to a location beyond the Confederate line. They moved over 18,000 cubic feet of dirt, which they spread across a ravine behind Union lines as to not draw attention.[xcvi] On July 23, 1864, they finished the tunnel and came up with a plan; two brigades would push into Petersburg via this secret hole in the Confederate defenses.

It took them six hours to place 320 kegs of gunpowder and lay in place a 98-foot fuse to light the kegs. Finally, on July 30 at 4:40 in the morning the Union army set off the powder kegs, blasting a hole 200 feet long, 50 feet wide, and 25 to 30 feet deep.[xcvii] The whole was filled with "dust, great blocks of clay, guns, broken carriages, project timbers, and men buried in various ways – some up to their necks, others to their waist, some with only their feet and legs protruding from the earth."[xcviii] At least 256 Confederate soldiers died as a result of the blast.

As the dust cleared, 10,000 black soldiers hurried through the mine and into the crater. Lee and his army stationed near Petersburg attacked troops both in and outside of the crater, causing panic and confusion. The Confederates overwhelmed the Union, and within a matter of hours, they had lost 3,500 troops to the Confederates' 1,500. The Union lost their chance to take Petersburg.[xcix]

Chapter 9 – The Final Fight

The war between the Union and the Confederacy was dragging on into its third year. With no end in sight, the Union went on the offensive in Virginia hoping to force surrender. As the war moved further into the year it was through this push into the heart of the Confederate territory that the Union hoped to end the war and return the Union to unification.

Sherman Burns Atlanta

The Union army in Georgia was gaining ground. General Sherman had been fighting a long land war chasing Hood's army throughout the South. Finally, on August 31, 1864, Sherman had defeated Hood's army and pushed them into Atlanta.[c]

Sherman gave chase and cut the Confederates off north of Jonesborough, destroying the railroad tracks leading into Atlanta and cutting off the last supply line for Hood's army in Atlanta.

The battle at Jonesborough was a massive victory for the Union and a blow to an already weak Confederate army. Sherman pushed the Confederate forces into Atlanta, and with the push, the Confederate army slid closer to defeat. There was no doubt that soon the Confederacy would fall.[ci]

Sherman's goal was the total and complete destruction of the Confederacy. Every victory over the Confederacy was designed to have the maximum impact so that the Confederacy would lose supplies, soldiers, morale, and the faith of the citizens of the Confederate States of America. The war was coming to an end, and the Union along with Sherman was doing everything possible to shut down the Confederate army and make them want to give up.[cii]

Sherman's March to the Sea

After losing the Battle of Atlanta, the Rebel army headed to Tennessee through Alabama. General Sherman decided to split his forces. He gave 60,000 men to Major General George Thomas to meet the Confederates in Nashville. General Sherman took 62,000 men east to take over the major port city of Savannah in order to choke off a major supply line.

As General Thomas headed into Alabama chasing the Confederates, Sherman pushed his troops towards Savannah, instituting a strategy that would become known as "The Scorched Earth Policy." Whatever farm, hamlet, or town Sherman's army encountered on its journey to Savannah; they completely pillaged and destroyed. After taking every item of worth including livestock, food, clothing, and feed, every structure was burned to the ground.

The places Sherman destroyed had already been hit hard. With the majority of men off fighting the war, or in most cases having been killed in the war, the only males left were either extremely old or very young. This lack of resources, both in available goods and available workforce, made it nearly impossible for these communities to rebound. And, this was precisely what General Sherman wanted to happen. If the people had to rebuild just to survive, there wouldn't be time or fervor enough to fight a war.

It took nearly three weeks for Sherman to make the 258-mile march to Savannah from Atlanta, breaking the backs and morale of the Southern population along the way. On December 21, 1864, Sherman's army marched through the streets of Savannah, Georgia unopposed. There had been a garrison of 11,000 men stationed there to protect the vital seaport, but upon news of the swath of destruction Sherman had laid down, they fled the city with the news of his imminent arrival. General Sherman found 25,000 unguarded bales of cotton, which he instantly claimed for the Union, proclaiming them an early Christmas present for Abraham Lincoln.

After securing Savannah, Sherman's army turned north for Charleston, South Carolina. He continued his scorched earth policy through South Carolina, declaring, "This Union and its Government must be sustained, at any and every cost," even though the preservation of the Union was paid for with the lives and livelihoods of civilians of the South.

However, the fear of General Sherman and his policy helped end the Siege of Charleston. After nearly two straight years of shelling from the Union armies and their technologically advanced artillery, the besieged Southerners stood resolutely. However, with news of Sherman's ruthless army on route to the embargo-breaking port city, the remaining Southern troops in the city fled. They could endure exploding mortars, countless fires, disease, and starvation, but they withered at the mere mention of an almost mythological figure.

Fall of Richmond

In April of 1865, knowing that the Union was gaining ground and the Confederacy was running low on supplies and troops, they left Petersburg and Richmond, Virginia. The Union had broken the defenses in Petersburg and were about to overrun both Petersburg and Richmond. With little other options, Lee took all he could gather and called a retreat.

The Confederate army under General Lee attempted to fall west, hoping to reorganize with other units in that area. In Danville, on the road out of Virginia near Appomattox, Union cavalry overwhelmed Lee's army, destroying a large part of Lee's supplies. Almost 800 troops were lost along the way as the Union army repeated attacks.

Lee's troops were too tired, famished, and unsupplied to mount a proper defense.[ciii]

Finally, on May 9, 1865, Robert E. Lee surrendered to Ulysses S. Grant at Appomattox Courthouse in Virginia, thereby ending Lee's campaign and the war in Virginia.[civ] The agreement signed by both Generals was one intended to reunite the Union. The official surrender of the Confederate army under the command of Lee came on April 12, 1864. Once the soldiers, marching with tears in their eyes, had laid down their arms, the two armies sat together and shared food.[cv]

Chapter 10 – Reunited

With so many years of war hanging over Lincoln, he sought to find an effective way to strike at the heart of the Confederate states. While the Emancipation Proclamation had helped grant freedom to slaves, it was still far from the total destruction of the institution of slavery that many in the North had called for. Lincoln sought to push forward the 13th Amendment and to, at last, remove the blight of slavery from the face of the United States.

13th Amendment Ends Slavery

On January 31, 1865, the United States Congress passed the 13th which stated, "Neither slavery nor involuntary servitude, except as a punishment for crime whereof the party shall have been duly convicted, shall exist within the United States, or any place subject to their jurisdiction." [cvi] Finally, on December 6, 1865, the amendment was ratified by the states.

This amendment created a snowball effect, moving many to find ways to grant equal rights to those who were still considered second-class citizens and who were still limited by the words, or lack thereof, within the Constitution.

Second Lincoln Inaugural

With the end of the war looming, Lincoln was elected to a second term. This time he took an opportunity to orate a brief but firm speech, which was to be one of his last. On March 4, 1865, worn and tired from an entire term of war, Lincoln stood before a crowd at the Capitol's East Front and gave the following speech:

"At this second appearing to take the oath of the Presidential office, there is less occasion for an extended address than there was at the first. Then a statement somewhat in detail of a course to be pursued seemed fitting and proper. Now, at the expiration of four years, during which public declarations have been constantly called forth on every point and phase of the great contest which still absorbs the attention and engrosses the energies of the nation, little that is new could be presented. The progress of our arms, upon which all else chiefly depends, is as well known to the public as to myself, and it is, I trust, reasonably satisfactory and encouraging to all. With high hope for the future, no prediction in regard to it is ventured. On the occasion corresponding to this four years ago all thoughts were anxiously directed to an impending civil war. All dreaded it, all sought to avert it. While the inaugural address was being delivered from this place, devoted altogether to saving the Union without war, insurgent agents were in the city seeking to destroy it without war-- seeking to dissolve the Union and divide effects by negotiation. Both parties deprecated war, but one of them would make war rather than let the nation survive, and the other would accept war rather than let it perish, and the war came. One-eighth of the whole population were colored slaves, not distributed generally over the Union, but localized in the southern part of it. These slaves constituted a peculiar and powerful interest. All knew that this interest was somehow the cause of the war. To strengthen, perpetuate, and extend this interest was the object for which the insurgents would rend the Union even by war, while the Government claimed no right to do more than to restrict the territorial enlargement of it. Neither party expected for the war the magnitude or the duration which it has already attained. Neither anticipated that the cause of the conflict might cease with or even before the conflict itself should cease. Each looked for an easier triumph, and a result less fundamental and astounding. Both read the same Bible and pray to the same God, and each invokes His aid against the other. It may seem strange that any men should dare to ask a just God's assistance in wringing their bread from the sweat of other men's faces, but let us judge not, that we be not judged. The prayers of both could not be answered. That of neither has been answered fully. The Almighty has His own purposes. "Woe unto the world because of offenses; for it must needs be that offenses come, but woe to that man by whom the offense cometh." [cvii]

"If we shall suppose that American slavery is one of those offenses which, in the providence of God, must needs come, but which, having continued through His appointed time, He now wills to remove, and that He gives to both North and South this terrible war as the woe due to those by whom the offense came, shall we discern therein any departure from those divine attributes which the believers in a living God always ascribe to Him? Fondly do we hope, fervently do we pray, that this mighty scourge of war may speedily pass away. Yet, if God wills that it continue until all the wealth piled by the bondsman's two hundred and fifty years of unrequited toil shall be sunk, and until every drop of blood drawn with the lash shall be paid by another drawn with the sword, as was said three thousand years ago, so still it must be said "the judgments of the Lord are true and righteous altogether. With malice toward none, with charity for all, with firmness in the right as God gives us to see the right, let us strive on to finish the work we are in, to bind up the nation's wounds, to care for him who shall have borne the battle and for his widow and his orphan, to do all which may achieve and cherish a just and lasting peace among ourselves and with all nations."[cviii]

With this speech, Lincoln signaled his desire to end the perpetual war, spelling out his disdain and hatred for the institution of slavery. His words represented the moral high ground that Lincoln had not pushed as hard for before the war, and which he was no longer afraid to express, having experienced through the Civil War the exact opposite of the peace he had sought when he first took office.

Lincoln Shot

John Wilkes Booth was born on May 10, 1838, to English immigrants Junius Brutus Booth, a Shakespearian actor, and his mistress Mary Anne Holmes. More of his youth was spent noticing the rolling Maryland countryside than paying attention to his studies. When Booth was 14, his father died, and he decided to quit his educational endeavors and pursue the path his father and older brother had blazed in the theater.

After making his debut at 17, he realized he would have a hard time breaking free of the shadow of his older brother Edwin's acting career. However, through his good looks and animated performances, his reputation and roles grew larger. He took the leading role in a national touring company, and by the time the 1850s were over, he was making the equivalent of over half a million dollars per year in today's money.

As the Civil War started, Booth's distaste for abolitionists grew. He joined a group of men that formed a militia and marched to Harpers Ferry to revel in the hanging of John Brown. He then spent two weeks in Montreal, a hotbed for Southern sympathizers, while making plans on how to deal with the North, and in particular, the President.

As early as August of 1864, Booth and his conspirators planned to assassinate President Lincoln. He had envisioned many scenarios, including kidnapping Lincoln and holding him hostage in Virginia until the Union released Confederate prisoners of war and let them return to the front lines. Each time Booth planned to eliminate Lincoln, it was somehow prevented.[cix]

Finally, on April 14, 1865, Booth and his conspirators had their opportunity to act. President and Mrs. Lincoln, along with Ulysses S. Grant, were set to attend a performance of Our American Cousin at Ford's Theater. As he worked out his plan, Booth learned that Grant would not be in attendance and so he switched his second target to Secretary of State William Seward. Booth had planned for the assassins to strike at 10:25 p.m., and then ride across the Potomac into the safety of Virginia and the Confederacy.[cx]

The Lincolns arrived at 8:30 p.m. and sat in a box overlooking the stage. He and his wife were enjoying the show when Booth entered the theater headed up the stairs and slipped into their private box. As laughter rose from the crowd Booth stepped to the right side of Lincoln, pulled out a derringer, and fired, tearing through Lincoln's left ear and into his brain. Lincoln slumped over as Booth pulled a knife and attacked one of Lincoln's guests at the theater, Major Rathbone. He then leaped from the booth to the stage, reportedly becoming ensnared in a flag as he fell, resulting in a broken leg. Booth still managed to escape from the theater, hop on a waiting horse, and ride away.[cxi]

With what many viewed as a blow to tyranny, Booth became a hero to those in the South. Some thought that the Union would fold or back away from the Confederates giving them room to breathe, and possibly allow them to live as a separate nation.

Lincoln Dies

After the shooting, Lincoln was tended to immediately by a doctor who was in the crowd. The president was taken from Ford's Theater to a boarding house across the road. He was mortally wounded, but the doctor attempted to do everything he could to save the president. On April 15 at 7:30 a.m., Lincoln was declared dead.[cxii] A manhunt for John Wiles Booth and his conspirators was in full effect.

Twelve days later, John Wilkes Booth was cornered on a farm near Bowling Green, Virginia. Union troops surrounded the tobacco barn in which he was hiding, and set it ablaze. A gun battle ensued, and Booth was shot through the neck, dying before he could stand trial.[cxiii]

Johnston Surrenders

On April 26, 1865, the war moved further toward its close as General Sherman of the Union army and General Johnston of the Confederate army met in Durham, North Carolina. The terms were set according to the agreement reached by General Grant and General Lee at Appomattox just a few weeks before. Their pact allowed troops to deposit their arms and public property then given parole as long as they pledge to not take up arms. All private property is to be retained by officers and soldier and everyone is permitted to return home.[cxiv]

This surrender by the second largest part of the Confederate army numbers 30,000 troops and is a huge blow to the entire Confederacy.[cxv] As they surrender Confederate President Jefferson Davis meets with his cabinet in Charlotte and they disperse and make their way west of the Mississippi.

The End of The Confederacy

On May 10, 1865, Union troops raided an encampment in Irwinville, Georgia, and arrested President Jefferson Davis.[cxvi] He was taken into custody and not released until May 13, 1867.[cxvii]

On May 23, 1865, the Union army marched down Pennsylvania Avenue, cheered on by crowds of people along with the new President of the United States, Andrew Johnson.[cxviii] The war was officially over. The war that engulfed Lincoln's entire Presidency and cost him his life was won less than a month after his assassination.

On Christmas day in 1868, President Johnson granted amnesty and a pardon to Confederate soldiers and those involved in "rebellion." The rebels were required to take an oath to the Constitution.[cxix] Some Confederate Officers fled from justice and hid in Mexico. It is estimated that around 10,000 confederates went into exile in Mexico following the war and Johnson's pardon.[cxx]

While the actual Confederate States ended with the conclusion of the war and the arrest of Davis, there was still a movement of rebellion in the Southern states. It has permeated the culture of the South since the Civil War and has become a major part of Southern identity, so much so that the Civil War is often referred to as the "War of Northern Aggression" among Southerners. It is this view which has given rise to most of the conflict and race relation issues in the South for more than 150 years.

My Brother, My Prisoner

The Andersonville Prisoner of War Camp was located in southern Georgia. It was 1620 feet long and 779 feet wide, and originally meant to house 10,000 Union prisoners of war. However, within a year, it was holding three times that amount. It was designed to be a modern and efficient facility, but in the end became one of the most shocking displays of inhumanity in modern times.

Walking into the prison after being captured, the Union soldier would be given one rule and one rule only. Stay out of the dead line. The dead line was an 18-foot space from the walls of the stockade towards the center of the camp. Any prisoner that dared cross the line or even touch it would be shot dead by one of the dozens of gun towers on the walls that watched over the camp. You would tend to think that no one would be daring or stupid enough to try to cross that line, but with the conditions in the camp becoming atrocious, many did try and paid with their lives.

Through the middle of the camp ran a small creek originally designed to be used as the prisoner's source of water. However, as the ranks of the Union soldiers swelled in the camp, the small creek could not sustain the needs of the 30,000 men who occupied the camp at any given time. As the prisoners used the creek, the banks began to erode, causing about a three-acre pond to form in the middle of the already tightly packed camp. The prisoners began using the pond as their latrine. As the waste from tens of thousands of men began to accumulate, so did the number of bodies of prisoners that had died from diseases such as dysentery.

Soldiers began turning on each other inside the camp. A group of desperate men began stealing and intimidating their own in order to just survive. Another group of men with a shred of civility left stood up against the marauders and formed a judicial system inside the camp. They passed down judgments on crimes ranging from theft to murder. Their judgements were swift, and some men even ended up swinging from their neck by a rope.

Upon liberation in May of 1865, a diary was found of a Union soldier. Inside was a painstakingly made list of every inhabitant that arrived at Andersonville during his imprisonment. This list and the story of Andersonville were published after the conclusion of the war in the New York Tribune. The story of the horrific conditions and the inhumane treatment of prisoners shocked the nation, so much so that the list found was used to create a memorial at the site in Georgia to honor the souls who had to endure the darkest natures of man.

Chapter 11 – Post-War America

Union Reunited

The Civil War had served to preserve the Union, which was the main reason Lincoln went into the war. He had stated that he had no other desire than to save the Union. Freeing the slaves and enacting the Emancipation Proclamation represented secondary goals. The Civil War had also closed a chapter on the debate that plagued the United States since its founding as to whether or not states could voluntarily secede from the Union.

The Union was now accepted as permanent; no state may secede from it, and each state is a part of the nation as a whole. The United States would be a single and solitary nation under the same banner, comprised out of the many individual states. This has been important for the future of the country since, while each state has its own laws and regulations, they all subscribe to the law of the land, meaning federal law enacted through the power of the United States government.

Slavery was impacted during the war by the Emancipation Proclamation and the passing of the 13th Amendment. The legacy of the Civil War and its role in the 13th amendment and emancipation was huge, considering that over 180,000 black men served in the Union army, moving forward the need for emancipation in the United States.[cxxi] This change in the perception of African

Americans helped them to move northward from the South, transforming the cities of the 20th century and bringing freedom to millions of former slaves who might have otherwise died in the bonds of servitude.

American politics and the ideas of parties were changed after the war. Support of the Republican party rose, and it dominated American politics for decades. The Republicans were perceived to be the party of the North and freedom, while the Democratic party was seen as the party of the South and thus oppressive to minorities.[cxxii]

Reconstruction (1865-1877)

On March 2, 1867, Congress passed the First Reconstruction Act. The Act divided the Confederate states into five military districts and put them under the control of the military, with each district being commanded by a general. The state governments who were rebuilding were only provisional until they drafted new state constitutions and allowed for the enfranchisement of black males and ratification of the Fourteenth Amendment.

Reconstruction was a huge undertaking that changed the face of America. The blacks that were once slaves found themselves free, but without wages or jobs. Many went north to find jobs in the cities.

From 1865 to 1877, there were three monumental changes made to the United States Constitution. These were the thirteenth, fourteenth, and fifteenth amendments, and their inclusion changed the entire nation.

The Thirteenth Amendment permanently abolished slavery everywhere in the United States.

The Fourteenth Amendment provided that the rights of citizenship could not be denied without due process. It states, "All persons born or naturalized in the United States, and subject to the jurisdiction thereof, are citizens of the United States and of the State wherein they reside. No State shall make or enforce any law which shall abridge the privileges or immunities of citizens of the United States; nor shall any State deprive any person of life, liberty, or property, without due process of law; nor deny to any person within its jurisdiction the equal protection of the laws."

With this amendment came opposition, not only toward those who supported it but to those that it affected the most, blacks. In the South, there was stern resistance to black equality and Republican politics. In Tennessee, the Ku Klux Klan had been formed in 1866 as a social club, but quickly turned into a rabid anti-Republican and anti-black group with a membership of tens of thousands. The Ku Klux Klan used these numbers to murder black and white Republican leaders, burn buildings, and terrorize freemen.[cxxiii]

Following the impeachment of President Andrew Johnson, who had assumed the Presidency at Lincoln's death, a Civil War hero was soon elected President: General Ulysses S. Grant. While political victories were lauded in the higher strata of American society, freemen were being denied their rights. Soon Congress passed several Enforcement Acts intended to prevent election fraud as well as to "enforce the rights of citizens of the United States to vote in the several states of this union."[cxxiv]

Still, the rights of the now-free slaves were challenged, and Congress passed the Ku Klux Klan Act which sought to suppress Klan activities and, if necessary, gave the President the ability to suspend habeas corpus in areas in which the Klan operated.[cxxv]

Soon another amendment was passed. The Fifteenth Amendment specifically extended the right to vote to African American men. It states. "The right of citizens of the United States to vote shall not be denied or abridged by the United States or by any State on account of race, color, or previous condition of servitude."[cxxvi]

While these were important advances, the South still found ways to restrict rights of African Americans and to prevent enforcement of these laws. It would not be for almost another 100 years that the Civil Rights movement would again change the face of America.

In some parts of the country, the Civil War remains a source of pride. Many in the South feel that they weren't given a fair shake and that, had Lincoln left them alone and not threatened them in his initial inauguration, there would have been no war, and eventually, the Union would have reunited.

The cost of the war, however, was devastating, given the total of 620,000 men who had died during the conflict. The Union lost about three soldiers for every two Confederate soldiers, with the Union numbers at 360,000 and the Confederacy at 260,000. Even worse was the effect it had on the number of men in the country since about twenty-five percent of the military-aged males had been lost.[cxxvii]

Although the war was intended to unite the Union and the Confederacy and usher in "a new birth of freedom,"[cxxviii] the South, no longer their own nation, still had a long, hard road ahead of them. With the amendments that passed, and the Emancipation Proclamation the law of the land, the blacks of the South were for all intents and purposes free. However, they did not enjoy the same freedoms that others enjoyed. In the South blacks were denied rights through legal and political systems designed to keep them from gaining any ground. Although no longer under the conditions of physical slavery, they were kept in economic and political slavery, which left them as second-class citizens at best. The restrictions they faced included segregation, being denied the ability to vote, and even being brought up on charges that only applied to black people.

Conclusion

The Civil War was about more than North versus South. It was about freedom, rights, and government representation. With the rise of the Republican Party and the movement to abolish slavery, the Southern states felt a great deal of concern over the loss of their way of life. The Democratic Party of the South wanted to maintain its way of life, and when Lincoln delivered his first inaugural address, it was perceived as a threat to their lifestyle.

Secession came soon after, and retaliation against the North for what the South saw as oppression was also swift. The Union responded with political, legal, and eventually military acts to reunite the nation. The Civil War was the result of the actions and reactions of two ideologies that each believed had grown too far apart to exist within the same nation.

President Jefferson Davis and President Lincoln were two sides of the same coin. Both were leaders who wanted what they believed best for the people in their nation and were willing to use every resource available to do what they saw as right. Though the Union had marched into the Confederate states on a mission to reunite the two nations, the war was the worst conflict ever to occur on American soil.

The wounds of those years are still fresh in our collective conscious. Each side has their version of the war, each with its own heroes and villains. While there may always be some tension about the Civil War, it was a war that redefined the United States. The unity of the nation grew stronger as years passed, civil rights became available for more citizens, and eventually, equality under the eyes of the law became the standard.

There is no doubt that the Civil War is a touchy and sensitive subject. Often the Civil War represents slavery, suppression, and violence against African Americans. While those were some of the aspects of the war it was a war of unity. A war that was fought to lift every person, every man, out from under of the oppression of the past and to usher in "a new birth of freedom," which is precisely what resulted from the brutal, bloody, and savage four-year conflict we call the Civil War.

May the lessons enclosed remind us to be vigilant, to learn, to empower ourselves and others so that we may not repeat the sins of the past, but instead move toward a future brighter, bolder, and more magnificent than that which we currently know. Only through history and the gathering of knowledge can we hope to progress towards being as Lincoln said, "…better angels of our nature."[cxxix]

Here are some other Captivating History books that you might be interested in

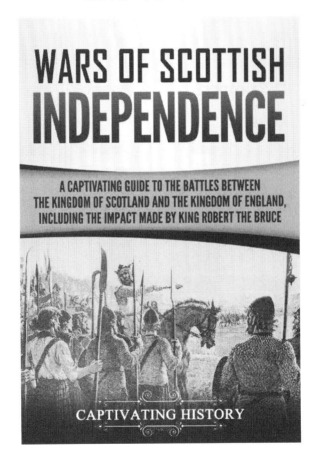

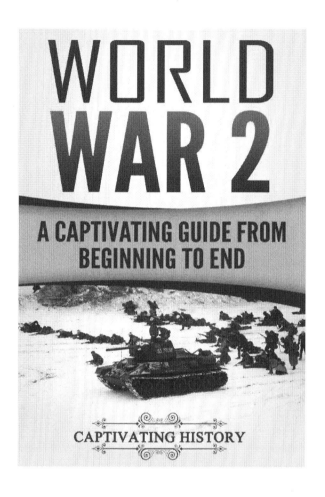

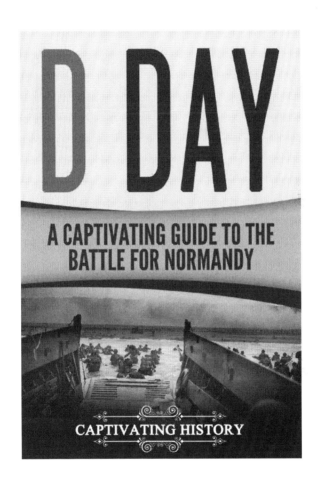

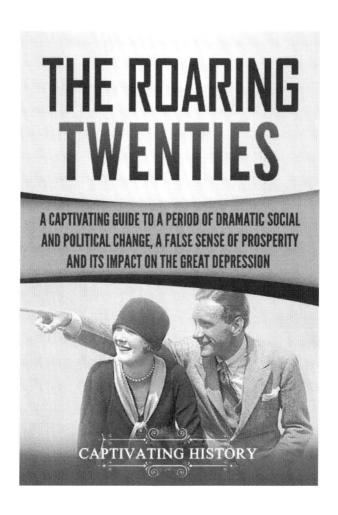

AFRICAN AMERICAN HISTORY

A CAPTIVATING GUIDE TO THE PEOPLE AND EVENTS THAT SHAPED THE HISTORY OF THE UNITED STATES

CAPTIVATING HISTORY

Free Bonus from Captivating History (Available for a Limited time)

Hi History Lovers!

Now you have a chance to join our exclusive history list so you can get your first history ebook for free as well as discounts and a potential to get more history books for free! Simply visit the link below to join.

Captivatinghistory.com/ebook

Also, make sure to follow us on:

Twitter: @Captivhistory

Facebook: Captivating History:@captivatinghistory

Works Cited

Avins, Alfred, comp. *The Reconstruction Amendments' Debates: The Legislative History and Contemporary Debates in Congress on the 13th, 14th, and 15th Amendments*. Richmond: Virginia Commission on Constitutional Government, 1967.

Brash, Sarah, editor. *The American Story: War Between Brothers*. Richmond, Time Life, 1996

Constable, George, editor. *Brother Against Brother: Time-Life Books History of the Civil War*. New York, Prentice Hall Press, 1990.

Cozzens, Peter, editor. *Battles and Leaders of the Civil War, Vol. 5.* University of Illinois, 2002.

Eicher, David J. *The Longest Night: A Military History of the Civil War*. New York, Simon and Schuster, 2001.

Katcher, Philip. *The Civil War Day by Day*. St. Paul, The Brown Reference Group, 2007.

---. *The Complete Civil War*. London, Wellington House, 1992.

Maus, Louis P. *The Civil War: A Concise History*. New York, Oxford University Press, 2011.

Stokesbury, James L. *A Short History of the Civil War.* New York, Harper Collins, 1995.

---

[i] Maus, Louis P. *The Civil War: A Concise History.* New York, Oxford University Press, 2011, 15.

[ii] Eicher, David J. *The Longest Night: A Military History of the Civil War.* New York, Simon and Schuster, 2001, 43.

[iii] Maus, Louis P. *The Civil War: A Concise History.* New York, Oxford University Press, 2011, 10-11.

[iv] Eicher, David J. *The Longest Night: A Military History of the Civil War.* New York, Simon and Schuster, 2001, 44.

[v] United States Supreme Court, et al. *The Dred Scott decision: opinion of Chief Justice Taney.* New York: Van Evrie, Horton & Co., 1860, 1860. Pdf. Retrieved from the Library of Congress, <www.loc.gov/item/17001543/>.

[vi] Constable, George, editor. *Brother Against Brother: Time-Life Books History of the Civil War.* New York, Prentice Hall Press, 1990, 32.

[vii] Constable, George, editor. *Brother Against Brother: Time-Life Books History of the Civil War.* New York, Prentice Hall Press, 1990, 33.

[viii] Maus, Louis P. *The Civil War: A Concise History.* New York, Oxford University Press, 2011, 19.

[ix] Katcher, Philip. *The Civil War Day by Day.* St. Paul, The Brown Reference Group, 2007, 17.

[x] Constable, George, editor. *Brother Against Brother: Time-Life Books History of the Civil War.* New York, Prentice Hall Press, 1990, 35.

[xi] Maus, Louis P. *The Civil War: A Concise History.* New York, Oxford University Press, 2011, 22.

[xii] Maus, Louis P. *The Civil War: A Concise History.* New York, Oxford University Press, 2011, 23.

[xiii] Lincoln, Abraham. *Abraham Lincoln papers: Series 1. General Correspondence. -1916: Abraham Lincoln, January-February 1861 First Inaugural Address, First Printed Draft.* January, 1861. Manuscript/Mixed Material. Retrieved from the Library of Congress, <www.loc.gov/item/mal0770200/>.

[xiv] Lincoln, Abraham. *Abraham Lincoln papers: Series 1. General Correspondence. -1916: Abraham Lincoln, January-February 1861 First Inaugural Address, First Printed Draft.* January, 1861. Manuscript/Mixed Material. Retrieved from the Library of Congress, <www.loc.gov/item/mal0770200/>.

[xv] Lincoln, Abraham. *Abraham Lincoln papers: Series 1. General Correspondence. -1916: Abraham Lincoln, January-February 1861 First Inaugural Address, First Printed Draft.* January, 1861. Manuscript/Mixed Material. Retrieved from the Library of Congress, <www.loc.gov/item/mal0770200/>.

[xvi] Lincoln, Abraham. *Abraham Lincoln papers: Series 1. General Correspondence. -1916: Abraham Lincoln, January-February 1861 First Inaugural Address, First Printed Draft.* January, 1861. Manuscript/Mixed Material. Retrieved from the Library of Congress, <www.loc.gov/item/mal0770200/>.

[xvii] Lincoln, Abraham. *Abraham Lincoln papers: Series 1. General Correspondence. -1916: Abraham Lincoln, January-February 1861 First Inaugural Address, First Printed Draft.* January, 1861. Manuscript/Mixed Material. Retrieved from the Library of Congress, <www.loc.gov/item/mal0770200/>.

[xviii] Lincoln, Abraham. *Abraham Lincoln papers: Series 1. General Correspondence. -1916: Abraham Lincoln, January-February 1861 First Inaugural Address, First Printed Draft.* January, 1861. Manuscript/Mixed Material. Retrieved from the Library of Congress, <www.loc.gov/item/mal0770200/>.

[xix] Lincoln, Abraham. *Abraham Lincoln papers: Series 1. General Correspondence. -1916: Abraham Lincoln, January-February 1861 First Inaugural Address, First Printed Draft.* January, 1861. Manuscript/Mixed Material. Retrieved from the Library of Congress, <www.loc.gov/item/mal0770200/>.

[xx] Lincoln, Abraham. *Abraham Lincoln papers: Series 1. General Correspondence. -1916: Abraham Lincoln, January-February 1861 First Inaugural Address, First Printed Draft.* January, 1861. Manuscript/Mixed Material. Retrieved from the Library of Congress, <www.loc.gov/item/mal0770200/>.

[xxi] Lincoln, Abraham. *Abraham Lincoln papers: Series 1. General Correspondence. -1916: Abraham Lincoln, January-February 1861 First Inaugural Address, First Printed Draft.* January, 1861. Manuscript/Mixed Material. Retrieved from the Library of Congress, <www.loc.gov/item/mal0770200/>.

[xxii] Lincoln, Abraham. *Abraham Lincoln papers: Series 1. General Correspondence. -1916: Abraham Lincoln, January-February 1861 First Inaugural Address, First Printed Draft.* January, 1861. Manuscript/Mixed Material. Retrieved from the Library of Congress, <www.loc.gov/item/mal0770200/>.

[xxiii] Stokesbury, James L. *A Short History of the Civil War.* New York, Harper Collins, 1995, 9.

[xxiv] Eicher, David J. *The Longest Night: A Military History of the Civil War.* New York, Simon and Schuster, 2001, 39.

[xxv] Eicher, David J. *The Longest Night: A Military History of the Civil War.* New York, Simon and Schuster, 2001, 40.

[xxvi] Eicher, David J. *The Longest Night: A Military History of the Civil War.* New York, Simon and Schuster, 2001, 40.

[xxvii] Constable, George, editor. *Brother Against Brother: Time-Life Books History of the Civil War.* New York, Prentice Hall Press, 1990, 39.

[xxviii] Stokesbury, James L. *A Short History of the Civil War.* New York, Harper Collins, 1995, 11.

[xxix] Stokesbury, James L. *A Short History of the Civil War.* New York, Harper Collins, 1995, 11.

[xxx] Maus, Louis P. *The Civil War: A Concise History.* New York, Oxford University Press, 2011, 25.

[xxxi] Maus, Louis P. *The Civil War: A Concise History.* New York, Oxford University Press, 2011, 27.

[xxxii] Constable, George, editor. *Brother Against Brother: Time-Life Books History of the Civil War.* New York, Prentice Hall Press, 1990, 41-42.

[xxxiii] Eicher, David J. *The Longest Night: A Military History of the Civil War.* New York, Simon and Schuster, 2001, 55.

[xxxiv] Stokesbury, James L. *A Short History of the Civil War.* New York, Harper Collins, 1995, 37.

[xxxv] Stokesbury, James L. *A Short History of the Civil War.* New York, Harper Collins, 1995, 44.

[xxxvi] Constable, George, editor. *Brother Against Brother: Time-Life Books History of the Civil War.* New York, Prentice Hall Press, 1990, 55.

[xxxvii] Constable, George, editor. *Brother Against Brother: Time-Life Books History of the Civil War.* New York, Prentice Hall Press, 1990, 59.

xxxviii Constable, George, editor. *Brother Against Brother: Time-Life Books History of the Civil War.* New York, Prentice Hall Press, 1990, 59.

xxxix Katcher, Philip. *The Civil War Day by Day.* St. Paul, The Brown Reference Group, 2007, 29.

xl Katcher, Philip. *The Civil War Day by Day.* St. Paul, The Brown Reference Group, 2007, 29.

xli Eicher, David J. *The Longest Night: A Military History of the Civil War.* New York, Simon and Schuster, 2001, 197.

xlii Constable, George, editor. *Brother Against Brother: Time-Life Books History of the Civil War.* New York, Prentice Hall Press, 1990, 79.

xliii Eicher, David J. *The Longest Night: A Military History of the Civil War.* New York, Simon and Schuster, 2001, 228.

xliv Eicher, David J. *The Longest Night: A Military History of the Civil War.* New York, Simon and Schuster, 2001, 228-229.

xlv Stokesbury, James L. *A Short History of the Civil War.* New York, Harper Collins, 1995, 72.

xlvi Eicher, David J. *The Longest Night: A Military History of the Civil War.* New York, Simon and Schuster, 2001, 230-231.

xlvii Constable, George, editor. *Brother Against Brother: Time-Life Books History of the Civil War.* New York, Prentice Hall Press, 1990, 118.

xlviii Stokesbury, James L. *A Short History of the Civil War.* New York, Harper Collins, 1995, 91.

xlix Constable, George, editor. *Brother Against Brother: Time-Life Books History of the Civil War.* New York, Prentice Hall Press, 1990, 120.

l Constable, George, editor. *Brother Against Brother: Time-Life Books History of the Civil War.* New York, Prentice Hall Press, 1990, 121.

li Constable, George, editor. *Brother Against Brother: Time-Life Books History of the Civil War.* New York, Prentice Hall Press, 1990, 122.

lii Stokesbury, James L. *A Short History of the Civil War.* New York, Harper Collins, 1995, 92.

liii Brash, Sarah, editor. *The American Story: War Between Brothers*. Richmond, Time Life, 1996, 181.

liv Stokesbury, James L. *A Short History of the Civil War*. New York, Harper Collins, 1995, 95.

lv Constable, George, editor. *Brother Against Brother: Time-Life Books History of the Civil War*. New York, Prentice Hall Press, 1990, 136.

lvi Stokesbury, James L. *A Short History of the Civil War*. New York, Harper Collins, 1995, 96.

lvii Constable, George, editor. *Brother Against Brother: Time-Life Books History of the Civil War*. New York, Prentice Hall Press, 1990, 137.

lviii Eicher, David J. *The Longest Night: A Military History of the Civil War*. New York, Simon and Schuster, 2001, 340.

lix Constable, George, editor. *Brother Against Brother: Time-Life Books History of the Civil War*. New York, Prentice Hall Press, 1990, 143.

lx Constable, George, editor. *Brother Against Brother: Time-Life Books History of the Civil War*. New York, Prentice Hall Press, 1990, 142-143.

lxi Eicher, David J. *The Longest Night: A Military History of the Civil War*. New York, Simon and Schuster, 2001, 353.

lxii Constable, George, editor. *Brother Against Brother: Time-Life Books History of the Civil War*. New York, Prentice Hall Press, 1990, 146.

lxiii Constable, George, editor. *Brother Against Brother: Time-Life Books History of the Civil War*. New York, Prentice Hall Press, 1990, 147.

lxiv Constable, George, editor. *Brother Against Brother: Time-Life Books History of the Civil War*. New York, Prentice Hall Press, 1990, 150.

lxv Constable, George, editor. *Brother Against Brother: Time-Life Books History of the Civil War*. New York, Prentice Hall Press, 1990, 150.

lxvi Eicher, David J. *The Longest Night: A Military History of the Civil War*. New York, Simon and Schuster, 2001, 396.

lxvii Eicher, David J. *The Longest Night: A Military History of the Civil War*. New York, Simon and Schuster, 2001, 399.

lxviii Constable, George, editor. *Brother Against Brother: Time-Life Books History of the Civil War.* New York, Prentice Hall Press, 1990, 199.

lxix Constable, George, editor. *Brother Against Brother: Time-Life Books History of the Civil War.* New York, Prentice Hall Press, 1990, 202.

lxx Eicher, David J. *The Longest Night: A Military History of the Civil War.* New York, Simon and Schuster, 2001, 404.

lxxi Eicher, David J. *The Longest Night: A Military History of the Civil War.* New York, Simon and Schuster, 2001, 405.

lxxii Stokesbury, James L. *A Short History of the Civil War.* New York, Harper Collins, 1995, 134.

lxxiii Katcher, Philip. *The Civil War Day by Day.* St. Paul, The Brown Reference Group, 2007, 82.

lxxiv Katcher, Philip. *The Civil War Day by Day.* St. Paul, The Brown Reference Group, 2007, 84.

lxxv Maus, Louis P. *The Civil War: A Concise History.* New York, Oxford University Press, 2011, 56.

lxxvi Constable, George, editor. *Brother Against Brother: Time-Life Books History of the Civil War.* New York, Prentice Hall Press, 1990, 237.

lxxvii Eicher, David J. *The Longest Night: A Military History of the Civil War.* New York, Simon and Schuster, 2001, 474.

lxxviii Stokesbury, James L. *A Short History of the Civil War.* New York, Harper Collins, 1995, 158.

lxxix Constable, George, editor. *Brother Against Brother: Time-Life Books History of the Civil War.* New York, Prentice Hall Press, 1990, 216.

lxxx Brash, Sarah, editor. *The American Story: War Between Brothers.* Richmond, Time Life, 1996, 181.

lxxxi Stokesbury, James L. *A Short History of the Civil War.* New York, Harper Collins, 1995, 158.

lxxxii Constable, George, editor. *Brother Against Brother: Time-Life Books History of the Civil War.* New York, Prentice Hall Press, 1990, 258.

[lxxxiii] Eicher, David J. *The Longest Night: A Military History of the Civil War.* New York, Simon and Schuster, 2001, 546-547.

[lxxxiv] Stokesbury, James L. *A Short History of the Civil War.* New York, Harper Collins, 1995, 170.

[lxxxv] Brash, Sarah, editor. *The American Story: War Between Brothers.* Richmond, Time Life, 1996, 181.

[lxxxvi] Stokesbury, James L. *A Short History of the Civil War.* New York, Harper Collins, 1995, 99.

[lxxxvii] Stokesbury, James L. *A Short History of the Civil War.* New York, Harper Collins, 1995, 148.

[lxxxviii] Constable, George, editor. *Brother Against Brother: Time-Life Books History of the Civil War.* New York, Prentice Hall Press, 1990, 248.

[lxxxix] Katcher, Philip. *The Civil War Day by Day.* St. Paul, The Brown Reference Group, 2007, 113.

[xc] Constable, George, editor. *Brother Against Brother: Time-Life Books History of the Civil War.* New York, Prentice Hall Press, 1990, 311.

[xci] Cozzens, Peter, editor. *Battles and Leaders of the Civil War, Vol. 5.* University of Illinois, 2002, 376.

[xcii] Eicher, David J. *The Longest Night: A Military History of the Civil War.* New York, Simon and Schuster, 2001, 622.

[xciii] Brash, Sarah, editor. *The American Story: War Between Brothers.* Richmond, Time Life, 1996, 181.

[xciv] Constable, George, editor. *Brother Against Brother: Time-Life Books History of the Civil War.* New York, Prentice Hall Press, 1990, 380.

[xcv] Constable, George, editor. *Brother Against Brother: Time-Life Books History of the Civil War.* New York, Prentice Hall Press, 1990, 380.

[xcvi] Constable, George, editor. *Brother Against Brother: Time-Life Books History of the Civil War.* New York, Prentice Hall Press, 1990, 382.

[xcvii] Stokesbury, James L. *A Short History of the Civil War.* New York, Harper Collins, 1995, 267.

[xcviii] Constable, George, editor. *Brother Against Brother: Time-Life Books History of the Civil War.* New York, Prentice Hall Press, 1990, 382.

[xcix] Constable, George, editor. *Brother Against Brother: Time-Life Books History of the Civil War.* New York, Prentice Hall Press, 1990, 384.

[c] Stokesbury, James L. *A Short History of the Civil War.* New York, Harper Collins, 1995, 284.

[ci] Stokesbury, James L. *A Short History of the Civil War.* New York, Harper Collins, 1995, 280.

[cii] Stokesbury, James L. *A Short History of the Civil War.* New York, Harper Collins, 1995, 284=285.

[ciii] Constable, George, editor. *Brother Against Brother: Time-Life Books History of the Civil War.* New York, Prentice Hall Press, 1990, 397.

[civ] Stokesbury, James L. *A Short History of the Civil War.* New York, Harper Collins, 1995, 319.

[cv] Stokesbury, James L. *A Short History of the Civil War.* New York, Harper Collins, 1995, 320.

[cvi] Lincoln, Abraham. *Abraham Lincoln papers: Series 3. General Correspondence. 1837 to 1897: Congress, Wednesday,Joint Resolution Submitting 13th Amendment to the States; signed by Abraham Lincoln and Congress, February 1, 1865. Manuscript/Mixed Material.* Retrieved from the Library of Congress, <www.loc.gov/item/mal4361100/>.

[cvii] Lincoln, Abraham. *Second inaugural address of the late President Lincoln.* James Miller, New York, 1865. Pdf. Retrieved from the Library of Congress, <www.loc.gov/item/scsm000283/>.

[cviii] Lincoln, Abraham. *Second inaugural address of the late President Lincoln.* James Miller, New York, 1865. Pdf. Retrieved from the Library of Congress, <www.loc.gov/item/scsm000283/>.

[cix] Constable, George, editor. *Brother Against Brother: Time-Life Books History of the Civil War.* New York, Prentice Hall Press, 1990, 408.

[cx] Katcher, Philip. *The Civil War Day by Day.* St. Paul, The Brown Reference Group, 2007, 183.

[cxi] Katcher, Philip. *The Civil War Day by Day.* St. Paul, The Brown Reference Group, 2007, 183.

[cxii] Katcher, Philip. *The Civil War Day by Day.* St. Paul, The Brown Reference Group, 2007, 183.

[cxiii] Eicher, David J. *The Longest Night: A Military History of the Civil War.* New York, Simon and Schuster, 2001, 829.

[cxiv] Katcher, Philip. *The Civil War Day by Day.* St. Paul, The Brown Reference Group, 2007, 184.

[cxv] Katcher, Philip. *The Civil War Day by Day.* St. Paul, The Brown Reference Group, 2007, 184.

[cxvi] Constable, George, editor. *Brother Against Brother: Time-Life Books History of the Civil War.* New York, Prentice Hall Press, 1990, 412.

[cxvii] Constable, George, editor. *Brother Against Brother: Time-Life Books History of the Civil War.* New York, Prentice Hall Press, 1990, 412.

[cxviii] ---. *The Complete Civil War.* London, Wellington House, 1992, 128.

[cxix] Eicher, David J. *The Longest Night: A Military History of the Civil War.* New York, Simon and Schuster, 2001, 844.

[cxx] Katcher, Philip. *The Civil War Day by Day.* St. Paul, The Brown Reference Group, 2007, 188.

[cxxi] Katcher, Philip. *The Civil War Day by Day.* St. Paul, The Brown Reference Group, 2007, 189.

[cxxii] Katcher, Philip. *The Civil War Day by Day.* St. Paul, The Brown Reference Group, 2007, 189.

[cxxiii] Maus, Louis P. *The Civil War: A Concise History.* New York, Oxford University Press, 2011, 85.

[cxxiv] Maus, Louis P. *The Civil War: A Concise History.* New York, Oxford University Press, 2011, 87.

[cxxv] Maus, Louis P. *The Civil War: A Concise History.* New York, Oxford University Press, 2011, 87.

[cxxvi]

https://www.senate.gov/artandhistory/history/common/generic/CivilWarAmendments.htm

[cxxvii] Stokesbury, James L. *A Short History of the Civil War.* New York, Harper Collins, 1995, 324.

cxxviii Eicher, David J. *The Longest Night: A Military History of the Civil War.* New York, Simon and Schuster, 2001, 622.

cxxix Lincoln, Abraham. *Abraham Lincoln papers: Series 1. General Correspondence. -1916: Abraham Lincoln, January-February 1861 First Inaugural Address, First Printed Draft.* January, 1861. Manuscript/Mixed Material. Retrieved from the Library of Congress, <www.loc.gov/item/mal0770200/>.